SF Express

John Ruszkiewicz
University of Texas at Austin

Maxine Hairston
University of Texas at Austin

Christy Friend
University of South Carolina

Longman

New York   San Francisco   Boston
London   Toronto   Sydney   Tokyo   Singapore   Madrid
Mexico City   Munich   Paris   Cape Town   Hong Kong   Montreal

Vice President and Editor-in-Chief: Joseph Opiela
Acquisitions Editor: Lynn M. Huddon
Marketing Manager: Christopher Bennem
Senior Production Manager: Bob Ginsberg
Project Coordination, Text Design, and Electronic Page Makeup:
    Nesbitt Graphics, Inc.
Cover Design Manager: Wendy Ann Fredericks
Cover Design: Kay Petronio
Cover Photo: © Isabelle Rozenbaum/Photoalto
Photo Researcher: Photosearch, Inc.
Manufacturing Buyer: Roy Pickering
Printer and Binder: Webcrafters, Inc.
Cover Printer: Lehigh Press, Inc.

For permission to use copyrighted material, grateful acknowledgment is made
to the copyright holders listed on page 243.

Library of Congress Cataloging-in-Publication Data

Ruszkiewicz, John J., 1950-
    SF express / John Ruszkiewicz, Maxine Hairston, Christy Friend.
        p. cm.
    Includes index.
    ISBN 0-321-08584-1 (spiral bound)
    1. English language—Rhetoric—Handbooks, manuals, etc. 2. English
language—Grammar—Handbooks, manuals, etc. 3. Report writing—
Handbooks, manuals, etc. I. Hairston, Maxine. II. Friend, Christy.
III. Title.
PE1408.R8685 2001
808'.042—dc21   2001038866

Please visit our website at http://www.ablongman.com

ISBN 0-321-08584-1

2345678910—WC—040302

Contents

Preface

Like most brief handbooks for writers, *SF Express* offers essential advice about mechanics, usage, and style. But it does much more. *SF Express* is designed to help writers today working in new environments with fresh attitudes toward composing. The fact is most of us are composing more and faster than ever before—in both our professional and personal lives. Sometimes we require general advice, sometimes we want precise guidelines, and sometimes we need to know where to go for more detailed information. *SF Express* addresses all these needs.

Drawing from the best-selling comprehensive handbook, *The Scott Foresman Handbook for Writers, SF Express* covers all the basics of grammar, mechanics, usage, and punctuation. It also offers a concise introduction to doing research in college and documenting work in professional styles (MLA, APA, Chicago, and CBE). A complete student paper provides a clear model of MLA style.

To put the chapter's content into a context writers can use, *Express!* boxes at the beginning of each chapter provide strategies for writing, thinking, and research. Specific guidelines and rules, amplified by numerous hand-edited examples, then follow. All of this material is presented in the friendly and encouraging style that has been a hallmark of SF handbooks for more than a decade. Indeed, *SF Express* may be the liveliest of the series.

Because *SF Express* assumes that writers now use computers and electronic networks routinely, technology plays an important role in most chapters. New or especially important concepts in electronic research, document design, and graphics are highlighted in boxes called *E-tips*. These *E-tips* cover everything from using Web search engines to choosing background colors for Web sites. An entire chapter on writing for the Web outlines the essential details of formatting and coding a site using HTML, including how to add images and links.

To be sure writers have all the information they need, each chapter in *SF Express* includes *Destinations*. *Destinations* are Web sites that cover a topic in especially comprehensive or creative ways. The URL for each *Destination* is accompanied by an explanation of its content to help writers decide whether it will be useful to visit.

Writers sometimes need a little encouragement or humor. So each chapter begins with a comment on writing, research, or creativity by people as different as Barbara Tuchman and Wayne Gretsky. A thumbnail portrait of each commentator gives this handbook a human face.

All these features are wrapped up in a bright and innovative package designed to help writers find information easily and to please the eye. The principles of document design we discuss in Chapter 5 are evident, we hope, on every page.

JOHN RUSZKIEWICZ
MAXINE HAIRSTON
CHRISTY FRIEND

PART ONE

Writing and Thinking

1   Critical Reading

"Be careful what you swallow. Chew!"
—GWENDOLYN BROOKS, poet

If you want to participate in a democratic society, you will need to sharpen your ability to think critically. As a student and as a citizen, you are bombarded each day with messages that try to influence you—to buy a new toothpaste, to give money to a certain charitable organization, to vote for one candidate instead of another. In college, you will learn to sharpen your abilities to assess these messages. You will learn to read and listen carefully, ask questions, challenge statements, and think about how new information fits into what you already know. The analytic and problem-solving skills you learn in college will serve you the rest of your life.

In college, you're often dealing with complex issues, using information from books, articles, and Internet sources. Thus an important part of becoming a critical thinker is becoming a critical reader.

EXPRESS!

To approach difficult or unfamiliar ideas, writing expert Peter Elbow suggests that you play the "believing and doubting game." First, read the piece from the perspective of a believer: Look for claims, examples, and beliefs that seem reasonable and persuasive. Write a paragraph exploring whatever seems most worth believing in the piece. Then read a second time as a doubter: Search for gaps, exaggerations, errors, and faulty reasoning. Again, summarize your conclusions in a paragraph. This process will help you become more skeptical of positions you agree with and more understanding of those you don't accept—in other words, it will help you become a critical reader.

a   Ask Questions

When you're doing research, whether it's for buying a car or gathering data for a term paper, ask the journalists' questions: Who? What? Why? Where? When?

Who wrote this?
What are the author's credentials?
Why did he or she write it?
Where did it first appear?
When did it first appear?

b Consider the Answers

Reflect on the answers to the questions you've asked. For example, judge the expertise of an author: A professional basketball coach might be an expert on motivation, but not a credible source in a debate on welfare reform. Think about what interests or biases may be concealed by an organization's name. What reputation does the organization have? Who are the people behind the organization? Weigh your sources, and verify any information that seems to serve their special interests.

E-Tips

Be particularly critical of information you get from the Internet. Much of it hasn't been screened, verified, or edited. Examining a print source, you may be able to evaluate its credibility by context and appearance: Does an article appear in the *New York Times* or the *National Enquirer*? Web sites are still new enough that many people haven't yet developed a set of criteria for determining their reliability. As a start, find out who posted the material on a Web site and what his, her, or their credentials are. This information often appears at the bottom of the home page or in the "About" section. Also, check to see if the site includes a note about when it was last updated; this is usually located on the home page. If a site purports to be giving the latest facts, but it hasn't been updated since 1998, you will know to check these facts in other sources.

c Evaluate the Evidence

Evaluate the evidence an author presents. In academic writing, evidence should be solid, verifiable, and factual. Ask whether the evidence is substantial.

How much evidence is presented? Enough to prove the author's case?
Where did the evidence come from? Wide-ranging sources?

How much of the evidence is anecdotal? How much is
   hearsay?
Is all the evidence fully and fairly presented? If not, what
   kinds of evidence has the author omitted?

Evaluate, too, whether the writer's claims are fully supported
by the evidence presented. Be especially skeptical when a source
proposes a simple solution to a complex problem.

d Talk Back to the Text

Critical reading is an active process. To get the most from
your reading, don't rely strictly on highlighting—talk back to the
text.

- *Use your own words.* When you arrive at an important point
  or get tangled in a difficult passage, translate it into your
  own words to clarify its meaning.
- *Track the structure.* Notes can also help you follow a text's
  structure. At crucial transitions, jot down a key word or two
  that explains where the ideas are going or how a new point
  fits in: "Example 3," for instance.
- *Respond with your ideas.* Don't just accept what the text says;
  talk back. Does a proposal excite or anger you? Write "Yes!"
  or "Bad logic." If the text raises questions, write them down:
  "But what about . . . ?" This kind of dialogue helps you develop your own perspective on the issues being raised.

e Summarize

The best way to make sure you've understood any text is to
write a summary—a boiled-down restatement of its content in
your own words. You can write a summary to help you study and
review important reading material in your classes; summaries are
also often used in research writing. When you write about research,
summarize material when it supports your thesis but doesn't include ideas you need to share in detail with your readers (see pages
54 and 58).

The length of your summary will depend on how you will
use it. A summary may restate only the thesis of an article in a single sentence, or it may present the gist of a whole text—its major
arguments and important examples.

- Restate the thesis in a sentence or two, using your own words.
- Divide the text into its major sections, and compose a sentence that sums up the content of each.
- Put the pieces together. Begin with the author and title of the piece, followed by your restatement of the thesis. Then add your summaries of each major section, in order.
- Revise and polish. If others will read your summary, add transitions so the piece reads smoothly, and eliminate any repetitions and minor details. Don't mix in your own opinions; keep the author's ideas and your own clearly separated.

If you use any source material word for word, be sure to place this quoted material within quotation marks.

DESTINATIONS

For two excellent online guides to evaluating Web sites, visit:

The Wolfgram Memorial Library at <http://www2.widener/edu/Wolfgram-Memorial-Library/webevaluation/webeval.htm>.

St. Louis University at <http://www.slu.edu/departments/english/research/>.

For comprehensive checklists on how to analyze written information, visit the Cornell University Library at <http://www.library.cornell.edu/okuref/research/skill26.htm>. ■

2 | The Writing Situation

"Writing saved me from the sin and inconvenience of violence." —ALICE WALKER, novelist

Writing is not a purely academic skill that you will leave behind at graduation. On the contrary, the writing skills you learn in college will help you participate more effectively in the world. In our information-based society, almost everyone writes. Through writing, people exchange information, debate issues, promote their own values, and advocate change. Alice Walker alludes to the power of writing in the quotation above; writing affects people's beliefs and lives, and can change the way a society or organization operates. Writing is also an important medium for intellectual inquiry. Many people use writing to work through their ideas on an issue or to help organize complicated material they learn at school or on the job.

Every writing situation differs, and thus there is no secret formula for writing well. Nevertheless, you will almost always write in response to some specific situation. Analyze your writing situation by asking yourself these three basic questions.

What do I want to say?
To whom?
Why?

Probably no other single habit will do more to help you become a skilled writer.

EXPRESS!

Some writing situations are defined, at least in part, by others—a letter to the editor may have a word limit imposed by the newspaper, a business memo must provide certain information requested by a manager. In your classes, the verbs your instructors use in assignments give you important clues about the types of responses they expect. Because these verbs describe patterns of thinking that can be applied to many situations, they are a helpful guide to actions you can take in writing both in and away from school.

Analyze: break an argument or concept into parts and explain the relationships among them; evaluate; or explain your interpretation or judgment.

Apply: take a concept, formula, or theory and adapt it to another situation.

Argue, prove: take a position on an issue and provide reasons and evidence to support that position.

Compare: point out similarities between two or more concepts or situations.

Contrast: point out differences between two or more concepts or situations.

Critique, evaluate: make and support a judgment about the worth of an idea, theory, or proposal, accounting for both strengths and weaknesses.

Define: state a clear, precise meaning for a concept or object, and perhaps give illustrative examples.

Discuss, explain: offer a comprehensive presentation and analysis of important ideas on a topic, supported with examples and evidence.

Review, summarize: briefly lay out the main points of a larger theory or argument.

Trace: explain chronologically a series of events or the development of a trend or idea.

a Topic

You may be assigned a subject or choose one; in either case, consider your own interests and questions to decide on a specific topic and approach.

- What does the assignment ask you to do? Make sure you fulfill its requirements.
- If you are writing for a college course, what specific aspect of the general course content do you find interesting? For any piece of writing, what interests you about the topic? What makes you curious? Why?
- What do you know a good deal about? What do you enjoy reading or arguing about? What community issues do you find compelling?

b Purpose

When you're planning a paper, think about your specific goals.

- Do you want to inform, persuade, or entertain readers?
- How do you want readers to respond? Do you want them to react intellectually, emotionally, or both? Do you hope to get them to agree with you, consider your new ideas, or join your cause?
- Do you want readers to take action? If so, have you made clear what you think they should do?

c Audience

To write effectively, analyze the knowledge, experience, and beliefs of your readers. Then tailor your work to appeal to them.

- Who wants or needs to know more about your topic?
- Is your audience a small, specific group or a more general one? What do you know about them?
- What interests the members of this audience? What is important to them?
- How much do they already know about your topic? What new information do they need? What questions will they have?

- Will any of your points conflict with their current beliefs or perceptions? How can you persuade them to consider a new point of view?
- What kinds of examples and evidence will they find effective and convincing? How much support should you provide?
- What tone of voice should you use? Formal or informal?

d Genre

Audiences tend to approach different types of writing with different expectations. Each type of writing, or *genre*—a lab report for a biology course, an editorial for the school paper, an essay for your English class, a home page for the World Wide Web—follows specific rules, patterns, or conventions. You need to understand the conventions of the genre you're writing for to reach your audience and achieve your purpose.

- What form should your paper take to reach your audience and fulfill your purpose? Will you write a letter, editorial, research paper, news article, essay, memo, email message, Web page, or other genre?
- Where could you publish this paper?
- Why do people read this type of paper? To be educated? Stimulated? Challenged? Entertained?
- What features or organization will readers expect?
- What style will readers expect? Breezy slang? Formal sentences?
- If this is a paper for expert readers, is there specialized language you should use? If the paper is for a general audience, how can you help readers understand unfamiliar ideas or difficult terms?
- Are there guidelines or samples you can consult?

Examine an effective sample of the genre to see how it is organized. An essay for a humanities course, for example, often includes an introduction that states the thesis, a supporting body that expands on the introduction, and a conclusion that sums up what the paper has achieved. A business report may require an executive summary that lays out the main points and conclusions of the paper, a description of the problem, a proposed solution, and a discussion of budget and feasibility. A Web site probably includes an opening screen that conveys introductory information concisely, hyperlinks to other pages that include short chunks of additional information, and links to other, external Web sites that are organized for easy navigation.

DESTINATIONS

For advice, templates, and links for writing letters to the editor, letters to legislators, editorials, press releases, and news articles, visit <http://members.home.net/garbl/writing/action.htm>. ■

3 | Planning

> *"Writing is easy; all you do is sit staring at a blank sheet of paper until drops of blood form on your forehead."*
> —GENE FOWLER, journalist and biographer

An hour or two of planning can save you days of writing on an unproductive topic. Finding a topic that will interest both you and your readers, focusing the topic to make it manageable given your time and length limitations, and developing a tentative thesis to direct your research and thinking are valuable preliminaries to drafting a writing project.

EXPRESS!

Some of the best issues for writing are unfolding right in front of you. Perhaps your school board is debating whether to require uniforms in city high schools. Or a branch of your town's library that serves a low-income neighborhood is slated for closure. Or local politicians are trying to figure out the best way to regulate the use of firearms by police officers. Because such debates affect your everyday life, you're bound to have a strong interest in their outcome. And when you concentrate on local events, expert sources of information—newspapers, community organizations, government offices, and interested citizens—are close at hand. Should you decide to publish your writing outside the classroom, you may even directly influence public opinion.

a Find a Topic

Be good to yourself. Choose an interesting topic, one that won't bore you. If possible, select one you already have some knowledge and ideas about.

List some possibilities.   Begin by listing some broad possibilities—as many as you can think of—that sound promising.

Think in threes. What three subjects do you like to read about—in magazines, newspapers, books, on the Web? What three do you know the most about—topics you often discuss, questions others seek your advice about? What three subjects are you most curious about? What three do you enjoy arguing about most? What three issues in your community do you care about most?

Next, run through your list quickly to reject topics if they seem too broad or you may not be able to find enough material about them.

Choose two or three ideas that seem both manageable and interesting. Talk with friends or classmates; they may see angles that haven't occurred to you or point out problems you wouldn't anticipate.

Browse online and offline.   If you don't have a subject yet, try browsing in the periodicals room or the new book section for topics that spark your curiosity. Look up your subject in the library catalog, computer database, or the directory of the Library of Congress (better known as the *Subject List*) to expand your ideas.

Don't limit your browsing to print sources—the Internet offers a multitude of resources and ideas for writing. If you have a general subject already, look for newsgroups to see what others are saying about it, and check for listservs you can subscribe to or whose archives are open for browsing by the public. If you still need a subject, browse the subject categories in *Yahoo!* on the World Wide Web; if you have one, try several different keyword searches, using a search engine such as *AltaVista* or *About.com*, to see which aspects of your topic seem worth exploring further. For more on online sources, see page 44.

b Focus Your Topic

Learn to write more about less. It's the details—the particular people and events—that will make your material come alive for readers. Instead of writing a piece on single parenthood, for example, you might narrow your topic to the difficulties of being an unmarried teen parent. Better yet, focus on whether providing day-care centers in high schools can help teenage mothers graduate and support their children.

Focus your topic by doing some preliminary freewriting, brainstorming, or clustering. Consult a library index related to your topic, for example, the multidisciplinary index *Periodicals Abstract* or a discipline-specific index such as the *Art Index*. In the index, scan the subcategories of your topic for ways to narrow your focus. To pinpoint specific issues for further investigation, ask yourself questions such as the following:

- *Questions of fact.* What is known about your topic? What still isn't known? Are some "facts" contested? Do facts seem to change with time?
- *Questions of definition.* How do the words you use to define your topic affect your understanding? How do your interpretations of the "facts" fit your topic into a larger category?
- *Questions of value.* Is the idea you'll be writing about a good thing or a bad thing? Ethical or unethical? Worthwhile or not worthwhile? Workable or not workable?
- *Questions of policy.* What should be done? What action should your audience take? What laws should be passed?

c Develop a Thesis

An essay's thesis is a sentence (or sometimes two or three sentences) that explicitly identifies the point of the paper or summarizes its main ideas. Your thesis statement is likely to evolve as you conduct research, draft, and revise, but often, writers construct a tentative thesis to help organize a first draft.

A thesis statement makes a claim that might be questioned or challenged. Ask about your thesis, "Does this thesis provoke a reaction? Could someone legitimately disagree with it?" If not, change it. Take a stand. And if an intelligent reader might respond, "So what?" or "Big deal!" sharpen the point you intend to make.

TOO VAGUE

A child who has a computer at home has many educational advantages.

MORE POINTED

Elementary school teachers are worried about the growing gap between children who have computers at home and can play math and reading games and those whose parents cannot afford such advantages for their children.

Ask basic questions about your topic, particularly How? and Why? Get to the heart of a matter in defining a topic. Examine issues that affect people.

LIFELESS

Child abuse is a serious problem with three major aspects: causes, detection, and prevention.

CHALLENGING

Prosecutors in some communities have based charges of child abuse on types of hearsay evidence that are now receiving tougher scrutiny from courts.

Your research will likely lead you to reconsider and limit your original thesis statement. Exactly how you limit it will depend on what your thesis promises. For example, you can consider this commitment in terms of whether you have started with a claim of fact, definition, value, or policy. As your project progresses, you'll want to refine your thesis to make a distinct and limited claim, and then follow through with the appropriate support and evidence.

ORIGINAL CLAIM OF DEFINITION

Zoos promote cruelty to animals.

CLAIM SPECIFIED AND LIMITED BY RESEARCH

Confining large marine mammals in sea parks for public amusement is, arguably, a form of cruelty to animals.

COMMITMENTS

- Find legal/popular definitions of "cruelty to animals."
- Define specific criteria for "cruelty."
- Examine what experts say about the condition of animals in marine parks. Or do fieldwork in such a park.
- Find statistics on animal health in marine parks.
- Find expert opinion on both sides of the issue.
- Show that conditions in marine parks meet (or do not meet) criteria for "cruelty to animals."

E-Tips

Unlike essays written for college classes, Web sites whose main purpose is to inform the public about an issue may well be organized around a simple listing of related topics:

> Child abuse is a serious problem with three major aspects: causes,
> detection, and prevention.

Focal points such as this statement can work well when you need to
divide an issue or idea into its basic components. If you were organizing a Web site around this statement, you would likely make some
fairly brief, general statements about the problem of child abuse on
the home page. The home page would then link to three separate
pages, one for each of the three aspects—causes, detection, and prevention. The simplicity of this design would help make the Web site
coherent.

d Plan Your Project

Most writers need some plan for organizing their ideas. For
a short piece of writing, you might make a working list of key
points, such as this student of literature did:

```
Thesis: Comic moments in Macbeth emphasize how

disordered the world becomes for the Macbeths

after they murder the king.

1. Comic moments after the murder of King Duncan

2. Comedy at the feast for Banquo

3. Comedy in the sleepwalking scene

4. Conclusion
```

As you think of specific subpoints and examples, you can add
them under each of the main points. If you are writing an essay,
think in terms of what your readers will need in the introduction,
the body, and the conclusion. For more complex projects, consider creating a sentence outline to develop a strong framework for
your writing.

E-Tips

If you are working on a hypertext project with multiple pages, storyboard your piece (see 5a) to help you visualize the entire structure before you start writing. First, make a sketch like the one below that shows how the various pages of your hypertext will connect to one another.

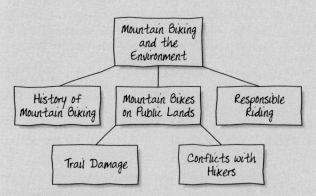

Second, sketch the layout of text and graphics for each page. Plan to include at least one element that will be present on every page to cue your readers that they are still in your pages. For example, the bicycle at the top of this page might serve as such an element.

DESTINATIONS

For in-depth discussion and numerous examples of how to craft effective thesis statements, visit the Writing Center at the University of North Carolina at Chapel Hill at <http://www.unc.edu/depts/wcweb/handouts/thesis.html>.

For an online outlining program and advice on transforming an initial outline into a finished paper, visit *The Arrow* at <http://www.nwlink.com/~cawilcox/index.html>.

For detailed information on Web site and page design, visit the *Web Style Guide* at Yale University <http://info.med.yale.edu/caim/manual/contents.html>. ■

4 Drafting and Revising

"It's not that the creative act and the critical act are simultaneous. It's more like you blurt something out and then analyze it."
—ROBERT MOTHERWELL, painter and writer

You can accumulate material even before you begin a draft. Start a computer file to store preliminary ideas, notes from your reading, quotations from sources, remarks from discussions, and your tentative conclusions about the topic. Over time you'll accumulate a surprising amount of prose that you can shape into a final text.

When you want to rework a draft, just save your most current draft as a new file with a new version number. Try out each new version while preserving all the work you've already done (you might want to use portions of an earlier version in your final draft).

EXPRESS!

Beginning to write can be difficult, even for professional writers. Authors have described the paralyzing anxiety they sometimes feel as they stare at a blank piece of paper or an empty computer screen. The delay that this fear can cause is so common that it even has a name: *writer's block*. What is the cure for writer's block? "Blurt something out," as Robert Motherwell puts it. Try some of the following ways to get started.

- Jot down a few key phrases: "Talk about yak milk"; "remember to refer to Rodriguez"; "make it clear that sitting in a tree for a year is a noble act."
- Write the same sentence over and over again: "I want to know what to write. I want to know what to write."
- Turn off your computer monitor and just start writing anything that occurs to you about your subject without looking at your words.

At some point, you will feel more relaxed and be able to start writing on your topic.

a Start Drafting

Experiment with the following strategies for starting a draft. You may find one that seems particularly productive, but even so, knowing several strategies will prove helpful since each project offers unique challenges.

- *Start anywhere.* If you feel most confident about an idea that will likely fall in the middle of the piece, start writing about that point. Don't waste your time agonizing over your opening.
- *Maintain momentum.* Don't criticize your writing or edit your work as you go along. Don't get bogged down in details.
- *Use writing that you did while planning.* You can lift whole sentences out of an outline, for example, and embellish them later when you revise.
- *Keep your readers in mind.* Write as though you are conversing with a member of your audience.
- *Track new ideas.* When you get a flash of insight or think of a telling phrase, jot it down so you'll remember it at the appropriate time.
- *Read to fill in gaps.* You may realize that you don't have enough information on a particular point to proceed. Research it.

b Explore Your Ideas

Use drafting to explore your ideas. Ideas are not fixed, and sometimes as soon as a writer sees an idea on paper, he or she begins to question it. Write down your questions and your possible responses in order to explore what you think. For example, you might look at an idea and ask, "But what if . . . ?" and then ponder different conditions or settings in which it might or might not be true. This process will help you refine your ideas and may change your tentative thesis statement considerably.

If you've done a lot of planning, you may already have completed much of this process. That's fine; every writer works somewhat differently. However, even a draft based on a detailed outline can go off in a new direction. Allow new ideas to occur to you; evaluate them when you have finished a rough draft.

If you get stuck and don't know what to write next, try various strategies such as freewriting (writing nonstop, even if you write nonsense), brainstorming on your own or with a friend or classmate, or responding to questions such as the following.

- What are some examples of this general idea?
- What is a general idea that might encompass all of these examples or anecdotes?
- What logically connects these two ideas?
- What other ideas does this idea seem to lead to naturally?
- If I believe this idea, what else must I believe?
- How does this relate to my thesis?

Questions such as these are helpful because they lead you to shift your perspective slightly. Often, all you need to get writing again is to examine your idea from a different point of view.

> **E-Tips** If you are writing a Web page, focus on your content in the first draft; don't start HTML coding until you have gone through at least one revision of your content. However, keep each page in a separate file right from the beginning—doing so will help you remember to craft each page as a separate entity capable of standing on its own. (Plan well: Put all your files for a project in the same directory; later, when you create links between the pages, you won't have to do as much typing.) You may want to start drafting your design at the same time as your content. However, if you are new to coding, keep your content and coding separate until you are sure your content is nearly final.

c Write Strong Paragraphs

A strong paragraph is unified, focusing a reader's attention on one main idea. It is coherent, indicating which thoughts go together logically. A powerful paragraph is also well developed, supplying ample details and explanations to make each point come to life.

Write unified paragraphs.   Individual sentences in a paragraph should not go off in their own separate directions. Every sentence should connect with the others to form a chain or web that keeps the reader focused on a central idea.

A *topic sentence* states this central idea. When the topic sentence comes at the beginning of a paragraph, it often predicts the ideas or supporting examples to come; when it comes at the end, it often sums up the details in a general statement. Here is a unified paragraph that begins with the topic sentence.

> The [Soviet] society in which I had grown up was one that officially proclaimed sexual equality and made it a point of great pride, yet stereotyped men and women in ways reminiscent of the American fifties. At school, we had mandatory home economics for girls and shop for boys, a practice no one thought of challenging. At the music school where my mother taught, to say that someone played "like a girl"—pleasantly, neatly, and without substance—was a commonly used put-down; in literary reviews, the highest compliment to be paid a woman writer or poet was that she wrote like a man.
>   —Cathy Young, "Keeping Women Weak"

Not all paragraphs need topic sentences. In reports and analyses, however, topic sentences keep paragraphs on track.

Write coherent paragraphs.
Every sentence in a paragraph should be a seed out of which the next sentence can grow. Always include a hint, a reference, a hook, or a repetition to help the reader link what you're saying with what has come before and what lies ahead.

Repeating key ideas establishes a motif for a paragraph. In this paragraph, Robert Coles repeats the term *idealism* or *idealists* four times, connecting that concept to the phrase *commitment to reform* in his opening statement.

> I have noticed, again and again, that those youths who are openly troubled about their commitment to reform as against their desire to live comfortable, respectable lives, are the ones who seem to last longest as active idealists. [. . .] Such youths state the obvious about themselves—that they simply cannot or will not shake off a youthful idealism in favor of various "practicalities," various "adjustments to reality," as pressed upon them by parents, friends, former college classmates, new acquaintances. Nor are such young idealists only to be found in the most prominent places [. . .]. Any number of dedicated idealists straddle the world of commerce and philanthropy, and make a constant and personal effort on behalf of poor people.   —Robert Coles, *The Moral Life of Children*

Transitions—words and phrases that link ideas—help readers understand the connections between sentences.

If one lives in an affluent suburb, it's easy to get the impression that Americans are healthy. In **such** places, walkers and bicycle riders abound, and restaurants feature low-fat entrees. The truth is, **however**, that many Americans are not healthy. Thirty percent are seriously overweight, alcoholism is a chronic problem, and an increasing number of teenagers are smoking. **Moreover**, obesity among children is increasing rapidly.

Transitional Terms

Similarity: although, in addition, likewise, moreover, similarly, such, yet

Contrast: however, instead, nevertheless, although, in spite of, on the other hand, not only

Sequence: after, before, later, now, subsequently, then, henceforth, first, second, finally

Cause and effect: as a result, because, consequently, for, since, therefore, thus

Others: personal pronouns such as *he, she,* and *they*
demonstrative pronouns such as *this, that, these, those,* and *such*
the relative pronouns *who, which, where,* and *that*

Parallelism—repeated grammatical patterns—is a forceful device for achieving unity (see pages 136–137). In the paragraph on Soviet sexism by Cathy Young (page 18), notice the series of prepositional phrases that begin clauses: "At school," "At the music school," "in literary reviews." These phrases tighten the connection between the individual sentences.

Develop the paragraph.   A well-developed paragraph provides enough reasons and details to make its point clear. This first draft doesn't.

```
Many people claim that they have the right to
choose whether to wear a motorcycle helmet.
But they don't consider the negative effects
of their decisions on their families and the
public. So mandatory helmet laws are a good
idea.
```

In his revision, the writer provides the explanation and evidence to support his point.

Many people claim they have the right to choose whether to wear a motorcycle helmet. In their view, they are the ones who risk getting hurt, so why should anyone else care? But they don't consider the negative effects of their decisions on others. First, their families will suffer. According to the National Highway Traffic Safety Administration, motorcyclists are about 20 times more likely to be killed in highway accidents than car passengers. As a result, wives and husbands are more likely to be left without spouses; and children will be left without parents. The public will suffer as well. The public-interest group Advocates for Highway and Auto Safety cites a study showing that taxpayers supplied more than $300,000 per person to provide long-term care to victims of motorcycle-related brain injuries; in 1993, motorcycle helmet laws saved the public more than $500 million in medical expenses. So in protesting mandatory helmet laws, motorcycle riders cannot argue that they're hurting only themselves.

d Review Your Draft

When you revise, you are not yet fixing or correcting your writing. Rather, you are shaping a work in progress, reviewing what you have written, and looking for ways to improve it. You may get new ideas and shift the focus of the piece entirely; you may decide to cut, expand, and reorganize on a large scale. At this point, don't tinker. THINK BIG.

- If possible, set the piece aside for a few days before rereading it, so you can view it more objectively.
- Review the assignment, as well as any feedback you have received from your instructor and colleagues. Ask yourself frankly how you feel about the paper. What's good that you definitely want to keep? Where does it seem weak?

- Create a simple outline that includes the thesis, the topic sentence or main idea of each paragraph, and the concluding idea. Check this bare-bones structure. First, does the draft hang together logically? If it doesn't, examine your concluding idea. Does it reveal a new intention that you discovered through drafting? You may want to begin with this point in your next draft. Second, consider the audience for your piece. If they read only the outline, would they understand all your main points? Would they understand the significance of these points to your thesis? If not, sketch in what other kinds of information you need to add to make your main points clear and their connection to your thesis obvious.
- Consider now a bold option: Should you write an entirely new draft? Starting a second time from scratch may be easier than repairing a draft that just won't work.

E-Tips

When checking the draft pages of a Web project, keep in mind that your readers may choose to visit your pages in any order. Make sure that each page stands on its own, content-wise, and doesn't depend on another page readers may not have visited.

e   Create a Revision Plan

If you find you have a workable first draft, go through this list systematically to decide what you should revise. As you check each aspect of your writing, take notes on the areas that need improvement and, especially, any specific ideas you have for revising.

Purpose

- If someone else read your draft, would he or she immediately understand what you're trying to achieve?
- Did you clearly state in the first paragraph or two what you intend to do?
- Does the draft develop all the main points you intended to make?

Audience

- Who are your readers? What will they want from your piece?
- Have you covered any material already familiar to your readers?

- Have you left important concepts unexplained or important terms undefined?
- Have you used language your readers will understand?

Commitment

- What exactly did you promise readers at the beginning of the paper? Did you fulfill those promises?
- Did you support all the claims you made in your thesis?
- Does your conclusion agree with your opening?

Focus

- Are you generalizing about your topic instead of stating specific positions?
- Have you relied mostly on common knowledge? If so, your piece may lack credibility.
- Have you supported your ideas with sufficient evidence and examples?

Organization

- Does your piece focus on a point or state a thesis? Does it then develop that point significantly?
- Do the transitions move readers sensibly from point to point?
- Would the paper work better if you moved some paragraphs around and thus changed your emphasis?

Proportions

- Are the parts out of proportion? For example, is the beginning much more detailed than the rest?
- Can your readers tell what points are most important by the amount of attention you've given to them?
- Does the paper build toward the most important point?

f Edit and Proofread

When you have a strong second or third draft, you can begin to edit. Editing entails making small-scale changes that involve style, word choice, tone, choice of examples, and arrangement at the sentence level. Consult Chapters 18–23 when you edit.

Proofreading entails checking for punctuation errors, omissions, spelling mistakes, and lapses in standard grammatical usage. Consult Chapters 27–32 for punctuation rules, and Chapter 33 for spelling rules.

For Web projects with external links, check the other sites you intend to link to and make sure they are still active before you code the links. Check all your links once more before you turn in your final project. Web sites shift around with amazing rapidity.

DESTINATIONS

For comprehensive information about each stage of the writing process, visit the *Writer's Web* at the University of Richmond at <http://www.richmond.edu/~writing/wweb.html>.

For a discussion of topic sentences and paragraph structure, visit the *Writing Tutorial Services* at Indiana University at <http://www.indiana.edu/~wts/wts/paragraphs.html>.

For brief guidelines on how to respond constructively to a classmate's or colleague's draft, visit The University of Wisconsin-Madison Writing Center's *Writer's Handbook* at <http://www.wisc.edu/writing/Handbook/PeerReviews.html>.

For a beginner's guide to creating Web pages with HTML, visit <http://cpcug.org/user/houser/html/training>. ∎

5 Design

"You can have anything you want in life if you dress for it." —EDITH HEAD, costume designer

Design plays an important role in how readers perceive the information contained in any document, whether it is a research paper, a Web site, a church newsletter, a poster, or a résumé. A well-conceived design helps readers get what they need from the screen or printed page.

EXPRESS!

You may be tempted to "dress up" your document with a wide variety of typefaces, illustrations, vertical and horizontal lines, dingbats, and the like. Don't do it! Keep your design simple and strongly focused on your main point. Your design should emphasize your message, not obscure it.

a Planning

Start by visualizing the entire document as you want it to look, including its color scheme, to create a document that's easy for readers to follow.

Design for an audience and a purpose.   Every design decision should be based on what you know or can assume about your readers, as well as your own purpose for creating the document.   What do readers want and need to know? What do they value? What will catch their interest? What is your goal in creating this document?

Decide on the image you want to convey.   Based on your audience and purpose, what personality do you want your document to project? Serious and scholarly? Crisp and direct? Fun-loving? Documents project distinct images to readers. Such images can arise from the tone of the document, from its visuals and layout, and from the attitude and point of view taken by its author(s).

Examine effective models of your genre.   Each genre—research paper, Web site, résumé, and so forth—has its own conventions of format, tone, and style. Refer to effective samples of the genre you are working in to take advantage of elements readers will expect to find.

E-Tips   Survey your word processor's document templates. These templates follow traditional page layouts, so they provide a great starting place for designing documents, even if you eventually want a customized final product.

Storyboard your project.   Storyboarding is a process graphic designers and artists use to visualize an entire project before implementing it. If you're planning a seven-page Web site, take out seven pieces of paper, and, with colored pencils, sketch what you want each of the pages to look like. This process will help you explore how the elements of text and graphics will look in relation to each other. For example, storyboarding allows you to decide on the following.

- whether to use charts and graphs, and where to place them
- whether a newsletter should have two or three columns
- how the layouts of the front and back panels of a brochure will coordinate
- how the headings in a résumé should be laid out to organize your work and educational experiences

b Layout

First impressions matter. You want your document to make a strong first impression, so think about its "body language." Be sure your document doesn't appear crowded or lopsided and that your readers can follow the flow of information easily. Consider the following points.

- Leave plenty of white space in your document—areas where no text or visuals appear.
- Move readers from upper left to lower right—put key information at the upper left, and arrange supporting points so the reader's eye moves smoothly down and across the page.
- Group related information—use headings, lists, and boxes to organize information for your readers.

c Academic Papers

Academic papers follow the conventions of the documentation style used, such as MLA (Chapter 10), APA (Chapter 11), and CMS (Chapter 12). For example, MLA style requires the following formatting features.

- one-half inch margins at top and bottom
- one-inch margins at left and right
- double-spacing throughout, including long quotations and Works Cited list
- author's last name and page number in the upper right corner of every page
- title of the paper, centered, in the same typeface as the rest of the paper
- every figure (picture or illustration) with a caption below it, and a reference within the text of the paper

See pages 88–98 for an academic paper formatted in MLA style. Even if your instructor does not require you to follow a particular documentation style, you can use the MLA guidelines to make your paper easy to read.

d Résumés

Your résumé is a brief outline of your academic and employment history, designed to give a prospective employer an overview of your achievements, skills, work experience, and references. Take great care in preparing your résumé: Assemble accurate information and arrange it handsomely.

Résumés may be printed on paper or posted on the Internet. Companies may also scan résumés electronically to find key words that indicate that a job candidate has the credentials needed for the available position. When planning your résumé, consult these general tips, but also examine models of résumés to discover which organizational strategies will best suit your résumé (see Figure 5.1).

- Adapt your résumé for each position.
- Use headings and subheadings to organize your presentation.
- *Personal information:* For paper résumés, include your name, current address, and phone number(s), and the electronic address of your Web site, if you have one. For online résumés, include your name, email address, and the address of your Web site, if you have one—no phone number or physical address. (By law, you cannot be required to state your age, gender, race, religious or sexual preference, political affiliation, or marital status.)
- *Education:* Specify your academic major and minor and any honors or special recognition you may have received, as well as any course work relevant to the position.
- *Work experience:* List all of your work experiences.
- *References:* Indicate the placement service that has your complete dossier, or list your references at the bottom of your résumé if appropriate.
- *Scannable résumés:* Do not use images, italic or underlined type, unusual fonts, vertical lines, or multiple columns. Use specific nouns that describe your credentials instead of relying on verbs to carry your meaning.

Make sure your résumé looks attractive, uncrowded, and easy to read. Always send a letter of application with your résumé;

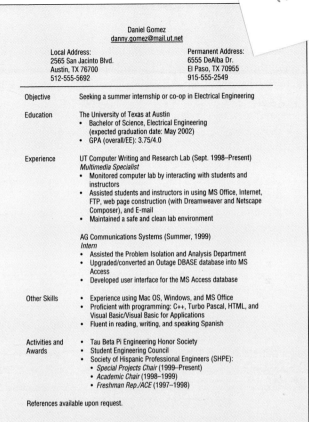

Figure 5.1   This print résumé emphasizes education and experience.

consult your university writing center or career services office for models and more information.

DESTINATIONS

For information on creating résumés, as well as how to post them online, visit <http://www.peachnet.edu/galileo/internet/jobs/jresumes.html>.

For an amusing discussion of bad Web design, visit *Web Pages That Suck* at <http://www.webpagesthatsuck.com>.

For a downloadable guide to the entire safe color palette, visit "The Browser-Safe Color Palette" by Lynda Weinman at <http://www.lynda.com/hex.html>. ■

e World Wide Web Pages

Online, readers tend to scan for information rather than read straight through, so you should provide plenty of visual cues that tell them what is most important in a Web site you create (see Figures 5.2 and 5.3). In general, ensure the following.

- the opening screen is concise and packed with crucial information
- the title is a clear description of your content; and for multiple-pages sites, each page includes the main title and subtitle for that page
- graphics reinforce rather than replace text, and graphics are as small as possible to avoid long download time
- links to other pages on your site are given on every page, and it is clear where links will take readers
- colors are "safe"—that is, they don't change depending on which browser a reader uses to access your page

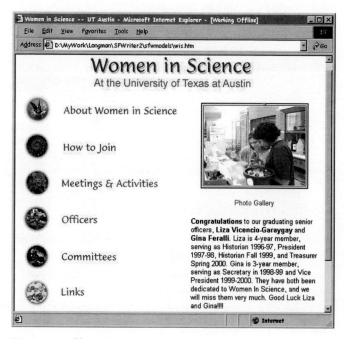

Figure 5.2   Homepage

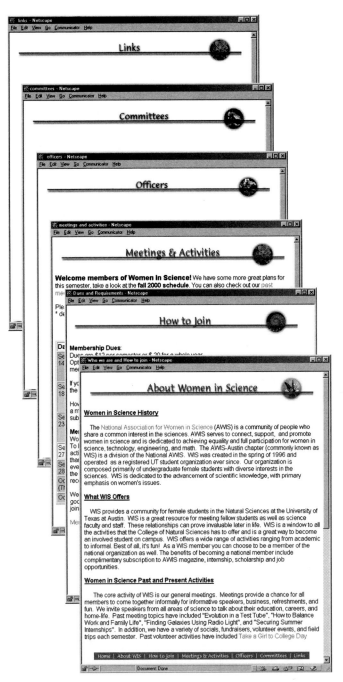

Figure 5.3   Content Pages

6 Writing for the Web

"I like to reminisce with people I don't know."
—STEVEN WRIGHT, comic, writer, and actor

Creating a World Wide Web site is similar in many respects to writing for print publication. You need to plan your work, based on your purpose and audience, and you need to write, revise, edit, and proofread your writing to be sure that it accomplishes what you want it to. Other aspects of producing a Web site are unique; we discuss them here.

EXPRESS!

Web documents use the HTML (HyperText Markup Language) electronic format. HTML tags tell Web browser programs how to display words and images and how to hyperlink separate documents to each other—the feature that makes the Web what it is.

To find examples of HTML coding, go to any Web location and from the "View" menu in your browser choose "Source" or "Page Source." You'll see a document containing the HTML codes for the page you were just viewing.

---

a Select a Method

Three basic methods of creating HTML documents require varying degrees of knowledge of HTML.

- HTML text editors require you to enter the HTML codes by hand. Although they don't have many user-friendly design tools, text editors are extremely flexible, since you can always compose with the latest Web standards and features.
- Visual HTML editors are also called "WYSIWYG" ("wizzy-wig") editors, which stands for "What You See Is What You Get." You don't need to know HTML because visual HTML design tools allow you to edit material as it would look in a Web browser. These tools don't always support the latest design features, however.
- "Save as" or "Export" HTML options in word processors and other kinds of software allow you to convert your work

to HTML using your program's menu options. This method is fast and easy, but the generated pages often need fine-tuning to make them appealing.

Combine these methods to take advantage of the strengths each one offers. For example, you might start a page by quickly exporting an existing document to HTML, and afterward add features with a visual editor.

b Choose a Format

Decide early in your design process how you want to organize your Web page: Will you create a single, scrolling page or multiple pages connected by links? If you have a limited amount of information to present—as in a personal home page, résumé, or brief report—consider choosing a single, scrolling page. If you have more than two or three screens of information, however, consider creating a set of pages connected by links. Most online readers don't like to scroll much beyond a few screens.

If you decide to create a multi-page site, arrange your information so readers can navigate the pages easily. You'll need to create a home page as the entry into the site. Material deeper in the site may be connected to the home page in different ways depending on your purpose and subject.

A hierarchy.   A hierarchy organizes pages into gradually more specific groupings. Readers find material by starting with general categories or topics and then working their way down to more specific information (Figure 6.1).

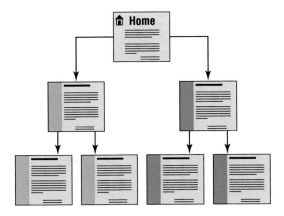

Figure 6.1   A Hierarchy

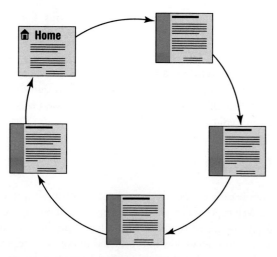

Figure 6.2   Sequential Organization

A sequence.   Sequential sites present readers with fewer options. Readers are encouraged to select "next page" rather than choose from a menu of options (Figure 6.2).

A hub.   A hub structure encourages exploration. The home page links to related pages that neither require a specific order of reading, nor fit into clear hierarchies (Figure 6.3). Readers can browse each page, going back and forth from the home page.

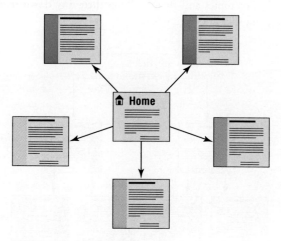

Figure 6.3   A Hub Structure

As you build your site, keep these general suggestions in mind.

- Make sure all pages link to your home page.
- Don't create "dead ends" that require endless clicking on the "Back" button to find new content.
- Use hypertext links to cross-reference material you discuss on a number of pages.
- As your site grows, consider providing a "site map," a special page that outlines the organization of your material.
- When you link to Web pages outside of your site, make it clear to readers that they are being taken somewhere else.

c Gather Your Materials

Assemble whatever materials you want on your site in electronic formats that are accessible to those browsing the Web. For example, photographs need to be "digitized" by a scanner and converted to JPEG or GIF files (two graphics formats that are Web-compatible). To digitize photos, make animations, or record voices, you'll need to use specific software programs.

As you collect your materials, create a working folder on your disk and place all your materials in it. When you're ready to publish your project, you can simply upload the entire folder to the Web server (see page 37).

d Draft HTML Documents

The way you draft HTML documents will depend on which method of Web page composition you use. Keep in mind the differences between drafting home pages and content pages. Home pages have less rigid layout standards, since you will use that layout only once on your site. Content pages, however, should use a consistent format to present the site's most important material. See page 29 for an example.

HTML is the nuts and bolts of the Web, so here we will take you step by step through the creation of a Web document using a text editor. Both Macintosh and Windows operating systems come with basic text editing software that you can use: *Simple Text* and *Notepad* respectively.

```
htmltemplate.html - Notepad
File  Edit  Search  Help

<HTML>

<HEAD>

 <TITLE>HTML Template</TITLE>
 <META NAME="Author" CONTENT="your name">
 <META NAME="Date of Creation" CONTENT="day/month/year">

</HEAD>

<BODY>

  HTML Template

</BODY>

</HTML>
```

Figure 6.4 Type the tags and words into your text editor exactly as shown. Later, the area between the <BODY> </BODY> tags will contain the main content for each page.

Use a simple template. All HTML documents have a basic structure, a required series of tags that tell browser programs necessary information about the organization of the page. Type the tags in Figure 6.4 into a new document using your HTML text editor. Save this document as "htmltemplate.html"—you will make a copy of this document every time you start composing a page.

Preview your document. Open the pages you have saved in your Web browser to see how they will eventually look once they are uploaded. (You will repeat this action as you draft your pages.) To preview your HTML document, open your Web browser, choose "Open" from the "File" menu, and browse for the file you just saved in your working folder. You should see something like the screen in Figure 6.5.

Learn HTML tags. Nearly all HTML tags come in pairs. For example, most of the tags you used to make the template include both opening and closing tags: <HTML> </HTML>, which appear as the first and last tags in an HTML document; <HEAD> </HEAD>, which enclose specific document information; and <TITLE> </TITLE>, which identify the title that will appear in the title bar on the browser when a page opens. Notice that the closing tag of each pair begins with a slash before the tag name.

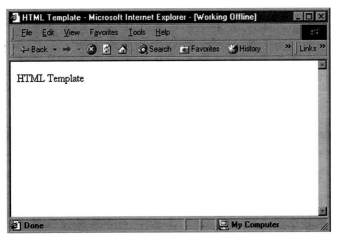

Figure 6.5 Notice how little of what you typed appears on the final product. Browsers hide all HTML tags, or convert them to special kinds of content, such as images or empty lines.

Some tags, however, don't come in pairs. The <META> tag you used in the template is an example. This tag provides extra information about the document, data often used by Web search engines to index the document once it is uploaded to a Web server.

The HTML tags that follow give you some basic tools for customizing your template.

HTML Tag	What It Does
<B> </B>	Boldfaces text between the tags.
<I> </I>	Italicizes text between the tags.
<P> </P>	Formats text between the tags as a simple paragraph.
<CENTER> </CENTER>	Centers text between the tags.
<H1> </H1>	Forms a level one heading—the largest HTML heading size. To vary the size, choose <H2>, <H3>, <H4>, <H5>, or <H6>. <H6> is smallest.
<A . . . > </A>	Hyperlinks the text between the tags. See page 37.
<FONT> </FONT>	Sets the font for text between the tags.

HTML Tag	What It Does
<UL> <LI> <LI> <LI> </UL>	Creates a bulleted list of items. Place the <LI> tag before each item in the list.
 	Inserts a line break. All text following the tag appears on the next line.
<HR>	Inserts a horizontal line across the page.
<IMG . . .>	Inserts an image on the page (see 6f).

e   Experiment with HTML Tags

Create a copy of the template you saved, naming it something meaningful. (For naming conventions, see 6h.) Open the new document in your text editor and change the words between the opening and closing <TITLE> tags to match the content it will contain.

Enter the text you've prepared for the page between the <BODY> </BODY> tags in the new document. (Or make up some text now with which you can experiment.) Just below the opening <BODY> tag create a page heading by typing your title between the <H1> </H1> tags. Format your paragraphs with the <P> </P> tags.

Some tags give greater control over the effects they produce by allowing you to set elements, or special attributes of style. The <BODY> tag, for example, provides an element to set the page's background color: BGCOLOR. All elements appear in the opening tag followed by an equal sign and a value (between quotation marks). Change the background color by modifying your <BODY> tag as follows:

<BODY BGCOLOR="TAN">

Always use straight (" "), not curly or smart (" "), quotation marks in your HTML coding. Experiment with the other HTML tags given above, viewing them in your browser window to see the effects they create, and check your HTML guide to find out which other tags have elements you can modify.

f   Insert an Image

The <IMG> tag allows you to add pictures to Web pages. Add the following text to your document, setting the SRC element to match the name of a graphics file in your working folder and the ALIGN element to RIGHT.

<IMG SRC="yourimage.jpg" ALIGN="RIGHT">

When you preview your page in a browser, you'll see the image contained in the file aligned to the right of your text.

g Add a Link

Using the <A> tag, or anchor tag, you can link your page to others, either within your Web project or at another location on the Web. To link to the Internet search engine Google, for example, you would enter the following text:

<A HREF="http://www.google.com/">Search at Google</A>

The HREF element allows you to specify an Internet address to which the highlighted text between the <A> </A> tags will be linked. To link to another page in your project, set the HREF element to match the name of another HTML document in your working folder. (In order to test your link, of course, you'll need to have created that other page.)

h Upload Your Page

As you have seen, you can view your Web page on your browser, but in order to publish it on the Web, you'll need to upload it. If you are composing a project for class, your instructor will give you uploading instructions. If you are composing pages for yourself or your organization, you'll probably need to establish an account with an Internet service provider, which might be your college or university. In any case, prepare your files for uploading by making sure they follow Internet file name conventions.

- Don't use any spaces or punctuation in your file names, except a period before the final suffix. You can separate words with underscores ("_") instead of spaces.
- Use the appropriate file suffix: ".html" or ".htm" for HTML documents; ".jpg" or ".gif" for graphics; ".txt" for plain text.
- Use all lowercase letters (suggested so you will not have to remember later whether you used any capital letters in file names).

DESTINATIONS

For more HTML tags, visit: Kevin Werbach's *The Bare Bones Guide to HTML* at <http://werbach.com/barebones/barebones.html> or *A Beginner's Guide to HTML* at <http://www.ncsa.uiuc.edu/General/Internet/WWW/HTMLPrimer.html>.

For a beginner's guide to creating Web pages, visit "HTML for Beginners" at <http://cpcug.org/user/houser/html/training>.

For detailed information on Web site and page design, visit the "Web Style Guide" at Yale University: <http://info.med.yale.edu/caim/manual/contents.html>.

To try out text and background color combinations, visit the Color Center at <http://www.hidaho.com/colorcenter/>.

For a downloadable guide to the entire safe color palette, visit "The Browser-Safe Color Palette" by Lynda Weinman at <http://www.lynda.com/hex.html>. ■

Related E-Tips

- Organizing informational Web sites: see page 12
- Making storyboards for multi-page sites: see page 14
- Drafting content and design separately: see page 17
- Making sure pages can stand alone: see page 21
- Using links as documentation: see page 58
- Determining chunk size: see page 139

PART
TWO

Research

7 | Finding Information

"If we knew what it is we were doing, it would not be called research, would it?"
—ALBERT EINSTEIN, scientist

Most college writing projects will require research both in the library and online. The sheer number of sources that seem to bear on your topic may be daunting; a wealth of material is available in print and online media. You can make sense of the riches if you are systematic and dogged in your efforts. Don't give up too soon when you can't immediately locate the materials you want. But don't be satisfied, either, if your initial searches produce more riches than you expect. Always push deeper into the archives, libraries, and networks.

EXPRESS!

Note cards are still a good tool for keeping track of bibliographical information. Each bibliography card should contain all the information you would need to find a source later, including the following.

- the author's last name and the title of the work
- the publisher, its location, and the publication date
- page numbers or URL for locating the source
- for electronic sources such as a Web site or newsgroup, the date you accessed the source
- for printed sources, a library call number or location

---

a Consult Library Sources

Your first priority is to become familiar with the libraries and research facilities on your campus. Begin exploring your research subject by examining the library's holdings.

Use library catalogs. Most libraries provide access to their resources via computers. Electronic catalogs can be searched by author, title, subject, and keywords.

DESTINATION

Some library catalogs can be searched via the World Wide Web; some also allow you to request materials from your school library using inter-library loan. For a list of online library catalogs, visit The *Libweb* index of "Library Servers via WWW" at <http://sunsite.berkeley.edu/libweb>. ■

Locate bibliographies. Bibliographies are lists of books, articles, and other documentary materials that deal with particular subjects or subject areas. You will save time if you can locate an existing printed bibliography—preferably an annotated one—on your subject. Useful bibliographies include the following.

> *Bibliographies in American History*
> *Guide to the Literature of Art History*
> *A Guide to the Literature of Astronomy*
> *Science and Engineering Literature*
> *MLA International Bibliography*
> *Using the Mathematical Literature*
> *Music Reference and Research Materials*
> *Harvard List of Books in Psychology*

Consult indexes, abstracts, and databases. Indexes—printed and electronic—list the journal articles, magazine pieces, and newspaper stories that cannot be recorded in a library card catalog. All provide publication information; some also give abstracts of articles or the articles themselves. Others also offer full texts of news stories, literary works, historical documents, and so on. Multidisciplinary indexes include the following.

> *ArticleFirst* (electronic)
> *Expanded Academic ASAP* (electronic)
> *Readers' Guide Abstracts* (electronic)
> *Readers' Guide to Periodical Literature* (print)

Discipline-specific indexes, both print and electronic, include the following.

Anthropology	*Anthropological Literature*
Art	*Art Abstracts*
Business	*Business Periodicals Index; ABI Inform*
Chemistry	*CAS*
Current affairs	*Lexis-Nexis*
Education	*Education Index, ERIC*
Engineering	*INSPEC*

Film	*Film Index International; Art Index*
History	*Historical Abstracts; America: History and Life*
Humanities	*FRANCIS; Humanities Index*
Literature	*Essay and General Literature Index; MLA Bibliography*
Mathematics	*MathSciNet*
Philosophy	*Philosopher's Index*
Psychology	*Psychological Abstracts; PsycLit; PsycINFO*
Religion	*ATLA Religion Database*
Science	*General Science Index; General Science Abstracts*
Social Sciences	*Social Science & Humanities Index*

DESTINATIONS

Two services that allow users to search large databases of journal articles are Northern Light <http://northernlight.com> and Ingenta <http://www.ingenta.com>. Downloading or printing a full-text article incurs a fee, but you can also use these services to locate relevant citations and then search for the printed articles in your college library. ■

Consult biographical resources.   For a good source of information about famous people, start with the *Biography Index: A Cumulative Index to Biographic Material in Books and Magazines, Bio-Base, Lexis-Nexis, Current Biography,* and *The McGraw-Hill Encyclopedia of World Biography.*

There are also various *Who's Who* volumes and dictionaries of biography. The two most famous dictionaries of biography are the *Dictionary of National Biography* (British) and the *Dictionary of American Biography.*

More narrowly focused biographical volumes include the following.

> *Dictionary of African Biography*
> *Dictionary of American Negro Biography*
> *Encyclopedia of Asian History*
> *Australian Dictionary of Biography*
> *Dictionary of Canadian Biography*
> *Mexican American Biography*
> *Index to Women*

Locate statistics.   Statistics about every imaginable topic are available in library reference rooms and online. Use up-to-date and reliable figures in your presentations. Sources include the following.

World Almanac (general)
Current Index to Statistics (general)
Statistical Abstract of the United States
STAT-USA (United States)
GPO Access (United States)
National Intelligence Factbook (world)
Handbook of Basic Economic Statistics
Survey of Current Business
Gallup Poll (public opinion)

DESTINATION

For statistics from more than seventy agencies of the federal government, visit *FedStats* at <http://www.fedstats.gov>. ■

Check news sources. The newspapers most widely available in American libraries are the *New York Times* and the *Wall Street Journal*. For information more than five or six years old, you'll need to use printed papers or microfilm copies.

For more recent events, try the following.

NewsBank, an electronic file of more than 400 American newspapers keyed to a microfiche collection
Facts on File, a weekly summary of national and international news
CQ Researcher, a source for background information on major problems and controversies
Editorials on File, a sampling of world and national opinion

DESTINATIONS

For very current events, you can search the hundreds of newspapers and news services currently online, including the following.

C-SPAN Online	<http://www.c-span.org>
Fox News	<http://www.foxnews.com>
London Times	<http://www.the-times.co.uk/>
New York Times	<http://www.nytimes.com>
Reuters	<http://www.reuters.com/news/>
USA Today News	<http://www.usatoday.com> ■

Check book and film reviews. To locate reviews of books, see *Book Review Digest, Book Review Index,* or *Current Book Review Citations.* For film reviews and criticism, see the printed volumes

Film Review Index and *Film Criticism: An Index to Critics' Anthologies* as well as the electronic *Film Index International.*

b Search Online Sources

To supplement the information you find in printed works, use the Internet to locate helpful information and to discuss your topic with other researchers.

Check the World Wide Web.   The World Wide Web provides access to an enormous amount of information. However, the quality of information on the Web varies a great deal: Some reputable sites offer information that has been evaluated and edited, but others offer slanted views at best. Approach the Web with caution as a resource for research, recognizing the differences in purpose and quality among sites. You need all of your critical powers when surveying Web sites for information. (See pages 47–51 for more advice about evaluating sources.)

E-TipS

Web search engines are the best tools for finding information. Each one works a little differently from the others, and all have particular strengths and weaknesses. Research your subject area on more than one search engine to explore their holdings. The following are the best-known search engines.

AltaVista	<http://www.altavista.com>
Excite	<http://www.excite.com>
Google	<http://www.google.com>
HotBot	<http://www.hotbot.com>
Yahoo!	<http://www.yahoo.com>

For advice on evaluating Web search engines and tips on Web search techniques, visit *Search Engine Watch* at <http://searchenginewatch.internet.com>.

Hundreds of reference sites have also been created by libraries, universities, and government institutions. Here are just a few places to look.

Argus Clearinghouse	<http://www.clearinghouse.net/>
Books on the Internet	<http://www.lib.utexas.edu/Libs/PCL/Etext.html>
English Server (CMU)	<http://eserver.org>
InfoSurf	<http://www.library.ucsb.edu/subj/>
Internet Public Library	<http://ipl.org>
Knowledge Source (SIRS)	<http://www.sirs.com/wrc>
Library of Congress Subject	
Guide to Internet Resources	<http://lcweb.loc.gov/global/>
The WWW Virtual Library	<http://vlib.org>

Enter electronic conversations. Some online resources provide dialogues about ideas or work in progress. You will find such resources on the Internet's Usenet newsgroups and listserv discussion groups as well as in interactions in MOOs. These resources let you question people actively about your research topic, but be aware that your contact may not be reliable. Corroborate any factual claims found online with other materials.

DESTINATION

For archived newsgroup materials, visit *Deja News* at <http://groups.google.com>. ■

c Understand Keyword Searching

A keyword search scans all the titles (and sometimes all the text) in a catalog, database, or on the Web containing the keyword(s) you have typed into a box or line on the screen.

Some electronic search engines use Boolean searching, a technique that gives you more control over what you are searching. Below are the standard commands.

AND   Using AND between keywords delivers sources containing all of the keywords you typed.

> Patrick AND O'Brian (delivers all sources containing both "Patrick" and "O'Brian")

OR   Using OR between keywords directs the search engine to find any examples of either keyword, allowing you to locate all documents that cover related concepts.

> Congress OR Senate

NOT   Using NOT between terms permits you to specify sites with one term but not another, excluding certain meanings of a term that are irrelevant to your search.

> Indians NOT Cleveland

( )   Putting parentheses around items allows for more fine-tuning. The example below locates documents that mention either Senator Gramm or Senator Hutchison but no other senators.

> Senator AND (Gramm OR Hutchison)

" "   Putting quotation marks around a phrase, such as "novels of Patrick O'Brian," brings up only items that contain the phrase in its entirety and narrows the list of items considerably.

Some search engines use plus (+) and minus (–) to direct some of the same functions. Take a few minutes to read the "help" files for indexes, catalogs, or Web search engines to discover the tools designed to maximize your search.

d Conduct Field Research

Conducting field research of your own can provoke insights you may not get from reading library and online sources—especially if your topic has a local emphasis.

Interview experts.   An interview with an expert—face-to-face, over the phone, or via email—adds credibility, authenticity, and immediacy to a research project. For email interviews, contact the expert and ask whether he or she is willing to help you with your research before you send a lengthy list of questions. For face-to-face or phone interviews, follow these guidelines.

- Request an interview in advance, and make it clear why you want the interview.
- Be on time for your appointment.
- Be prepared: Have a list of questions and follow-ups ready.
- Take careful notes, especially if you intend to quote the source.
- Double-check direct quotations, and be sure your source is willing to be quoted in your project.
- If you plan to tape the interview, get your subject's approval before turning the machine on.
- Promise to provide a copy of your completed paper.
- Send a note of thanks.

Write or email professional organizations.   Almost every subject, cause, concept, or idea is represented by a professional organization, society, bureau, office, or lobby. To look for Web sites, or for mailing addresses, consult the *Encyclopedia of Associations*.

DESTINATION

The U.S. government offers a wealth of information. Start your search at <http://www.fedworld.gov>. ■

8 | Evaluating Sources

"Read first the best books. The important thing for you is not how much you know, but the quality of what you know."

—DESIDERIUS ERASMUS, philosopher

The value of a source will depend on both its trustworthiness—"the quality of what you know"—and the way you intend to use it. For example, if you were writing a report on the official positions taken by the Democrats and Republicans in a long-past presidential election, you'd probably depend on scholarly books and articles, as well as newspaper accounts archived in the library. However, if you were writing about a current political campaign, you might read the views expressed in current campaign literature, recent magazines, and even Web sites and Usenet newsgroups. These sources might lack the authority and perspective of scholarly books or even official party materials, but they would still provide an excellent survey of political attitudes.

Even if sources can't be described as simply "good" or "bad" without considering their purposes, they do have strengths and weaknesses you must weigh when working on particular projects.

EXPRESS!

After you've decided a source is reliable and suited to the purpose of your research project, you should "position" it within your project. When you position a source, you identify its perspectives, biases, strengths, and limitations so that you do not misrepresent the information when you report it. Not all sources can be used in the same way. For example, some materials offer the most up-to-date and responsible treatment of a subject, while others have distinct points of view. Others might be "off the wall," but nonetheless make revealing points about culture and society. Positioning a source will help you stay conscious of the contexts that can shape and influence sources.

Positioning is more of a mental exercise than a written exercise. Still, the example on page 48 may help you think about what kinds of questions to ask about a source. See pages 52–53 for the short article referred to by this positioning statement.

**POSITIONING AN EDITORIAL TITLED "LEAVE THE PEOPLE HOME"
BY ALEX ROLAND**

"Leave the People Home" is an editorial that
appeared in USA Today on July 7, 1997, following
the successful landing on Mars of a research
robot. The piece, written by Alex Roland, appears
as a rebuttal to the paper's official editorial
position endorsing exploration of Mars by human
explorers. Owned by Gannett, USA Today is a daily
newspaper available throughout the country with a
predominantly liberal editorial page. It
routinely publishes counterpoints to its
editorials. USA Today notes that Alex Roland is
"chair of the history department at Duke
University, teaches technology history and is a
former NASA historian." Roland's academic
credentials and work with the American space
agency would seem to give him authority on this
subject. The editorial was accessed online on
July 7, 1997, for a Web project exploring the
pros and cons of a human mission to Mars.

a Evaluate Print Sources

Print sources are generally reliable because they have been
screened by publishers and librarians. But this does not mean they
are always the best sources for your research project.

- Scholarly books and articles are among the most carefully
  researched, reviewed, and edited sources, although they are
  rarely current because it takes time to prepare and publish
  them. Their authors are recognized authorities, and their as-
  sertions are fully documented.
- Serious trade books and articles are written for well-educated
  but nonexpert readers who wish to acquire more than general knowledge about a subject. Serious periodicals include
  *Scientific American, New York Review of Books, The New Re-
  public, National Review,* and *Humanist.*

- Popular magazines and books (print or online) tend to be less demanding and shorter than serious or scholarly materials. Their sources may not be specifically identified, documented, or linked. Some familiar popular magazines include *Time, Psychology Today,* and *Smithsonian.*
- Newspapers and news organizations (print and online) provide up-to-date and generally reliable information about current events, as well as many features chronicling popular culture and political opinion. Published daily or weekly, newspapers lack the perspective of scholarly works but play an essential documentary function. Most news sources have political biases that you should take into account.

b Evaluate Online Sources

New technologies mean that more and more sources come to you directly from their authors, unreviewed and unrefereed by publishers and librarians. Therefore, you must lean heavily on your critical skills to separate the good sources from the bad ones.

- Sponsored Web sites, created and supported by well-known institutions, organizations, and companies share in the credibility of their supporting groups. Thus Web sites posted by the U.S. government or by colleges and universities can usually be trusted.
- Online news organizations, such as *CNN Online* and *MSNBC,* provide up-to-date and generally reliable information about current events, popular culture, and political opinion.
- Individual Web sites are rarely refereed or reviewed by third parties who might take some responsibility for their accuracy. Confirm any hard facts in a second, more traditional source. When corresponding with an authority by email, be sure to record accurately both your questions and the expert's answers.
- Listservs and Usenet newsgroups can provide a way of learning quickly about current interests and debates related to your topic. As in any extended conversation, however, participants may vary widely in what they know; facts and figures may be reported unreliably; and the actual credibility of participants may be unknown.

E-Tips

> The Web is full of outdated sites, posted and abandoned by their authors. To find the date of a Web site's original posting or its most recent update, check the bottom of the site's first page or the "About This Site" section.

DESTINATION

About.com at <http://about.com> offers lists of reliable Web sites on a wide variety of topics; each site has been reviewed and screened by an expert in the subject. ■

c   Question Every Source

Examine each of your sources from several angles, using the questions below.

- Is the source authoritative and reputable? Reputable books, authors, reference tools, and Web sites will be cited by other reputable sources.
- Is the source stable and up-to-date? Generally, support your projects by the most current and reputable information in a field, but aim for a mix of sources—some classic works from the past as well as some current sources.
- What are the biases of the source? Almost all sources have political, social, or religious points of view that shape the information they contain and exclude. Sometimes these biases are apparent: the editorial page of the *New York Times* tends to be "liberal" in its politics and that of the *Wall Street Journal* tends to be "conservative." It may be harder to detect the biases of other sources, but be assured they are there. Ask instructors or librarians to help you select sources containing a spectrum of opinions.
- What commercial messages appear alongside of the source? It's easy to ignore printed ads in magazines, but Web sites are often so thick with ads that they can be difficult to use. Sponsored sites may also reflect the commercial connections of their owners, especially when news organizations are owned by larger companies with entertainment or other commercial interests. What appears—or doesn't appear—on a site may be determined by who is supporting the message. Be aware of such attempts to influence your judgment.

- How well does the source present key information? The design of a source is of greater concern with Web sites than with printed books and articles. A quality Web site
  - identifies its purpose clearly
  - arranges information logically
  - uses graphics to enhance its mission
  - furnishes relevant and selective links to other responsible resources
  - provides the identity and email address of the author/sponsor, and the date of the posting

Remember to consult librarians and instructors. These people often have the expertise to cut a lengthy list of sources to the three or four you should not miss.

DESTINATION

For a bibliography on evaluating information on the Internet, visit the *Information Quality WWW Virtual Library* at <http://www.vuw.ac.nz/~agsmith/evaln/evaln.htm>.

See also the Destinations on page 44. ■

9 | Using Sources

"It is curiosity, initiative, originality, and the ruthless application of honesty that count in research—much more than feats of logic and memory alone." —JULIAN HUXLEY, biologist

As you gather research materials, read them critically in terms of your research question or tentative thesis. Does a source advance your argument, fill a hole in your background information, or perhaps change your opinion? Approach all sources actively and intensely, reading them slowly, and then thinking deeply about their implications and ideas. This critical reading might—perhaps *should*—lead you to refine your initial thinking and do even more reading and research.

EXPRESS!

A good way to begin mining a source for information is to annotate it. As you read and think, annotate your sources—make comments, ask questions, and react to ideas, either directly on a photocopy, printout, or electronic file, or by writing your responses in a notebook. Annotation helps you to identify ideas and information worth returning to and, more important, to engage in a dialogue with the authors and sources you encounter.

When you mark key passages—with a pen or the annotation feature on your word processor—be sure to add a note to yourself that explains the importance of the passage or states your reaction to it.

a Paraphrase Accurately

A paraphrase usually reviews a complete source in some detail. When paraphrasing a work, you report its key information or restate its core arguments point by point in your own words. Follow these guidelines to prepare paraphrases.

- Put paraphrased material entirely in your own words, except for clearly marked quotations. Inadvertently copying the original author's words without quotation marks is plagiarism.
- Ensure that the paraphrase reflects the structure of the original piece and the ideas of the original author.
- Document each important fact or direct quotation with a specific page number from the source.
- Paraphrase only the material that is relevant to your research topic.

Reprinted below is "Leave the People Home" by Alex Roland, an article that appeared in *USA Today* on July 7, 1997. A paraphrase follows the article.

"Leave the People Home"
by Alex Roland

The debacle currently unfolding aboard the *Mir* space station argues against sending people to Mars any time soon. To think about a manned Mars mission now is like planning your next cruise during an abandon-ship exercise.

The problem is putting people in space.

All the really useful things done in space have been achieved with automated spacecraft controlled by people on Earth. The record is long and impressive—scientific probes to the planets and beyond, communications satellites, weather satellites, reconnaissance satellites, the global positioning system.

Two bad things happen when humans come aboard. First, cost increases by an order of magnitude, mostly to pay for life-support equipment and safety precautions. Second, the spacecraft becomes a lifeboat. Whatever mission it was intended to conduct—research, exploration, commerce—takes second place to saving the crew and returning them to Earth. The people, supposedly a means to some end, become the end themselves.

The *Pathfinder* spacecraft, due to touch down on Mars July 4th, is a case in point. At a tiny fraction of what a manned mission would cost (indeed, at a small fraction of the cost of a single shuttle mission), this resourceful spacecraft, and the roving *Sojourner* vehicle it carries, will do more and better research than astronauts could do. Machines can reach more places, stay longer, and take more risks.

But machines, you say, are not as dramatic, not as interesting as people. It is not the practicality of a manned Mars mission that appeals, but the romance. Sending people to Mars is a feel-good mission that speaks to the basic human longing to explore.

Well, our next feel-good mission is already booked.

Later this year, components of the international space station are scheduled to rocket into orbit. In 1999, three years before construction is complete, people will begin to inhabit it permanently. If it proves useful, more durable and safer than *Mir*, there will be plenty of time and a better argument for sending people to Mars.

For now, however, we have all we can do to find a reason, a budget, and a technology to keep people in orbit.

PARAPHRASE

Recent problems on the Russian space station *Mir* make it clear why a human mission to Mars may not be a good idea: People in space cause problems that robots don't. Automated spacecraft perform almost all the really important work in space (communications, weather satellites, global positioning). Spacecraft that carry astronauts must also take along everything that keeps them alive, adding tremendously to the weight and complexity of the missions. When something goes wrong, the whole project is jeopardized by the need to preserve the lives of the astronauts. The Mars *Pathfinder* expedition, in contrast, was accomplished far more cheaply than even a routine space shuttle launch and yet can do more science over the long term than a human expedition because it isn't as vulnerable. We may like the adventure and romance that comes along with human space exploration, and we'll have that with the international space station. But humans in space are an expensive and possibly unnecessary luxury.

b Summarize Clearly

A summary captures the gist of a source or some portion of it, boiling it down to a few words or sentences. Summarize those materials that support your thesis but do not provide an extended argument or idea you need to share with readers.

When summarizing a source, identify the key facts or ideas and put them in your own words. In long sources, look for topic ideas in each major section. Then assemble these ideas into a short, coherent statement about the whole piece, only as detailed as you need for your project. For example, here is a summary of the source on page 52.

SUMMARY

Alex Roland, chair of history at Duke University and a former historian at NASA, argues that using automated spacecraft to explore planets makes better sense than sending people because humans in space increase costs and risks and reduce the potential for long-term, productive science.

c Use Direct Quotations Carefully

A direct quotation is any material repeated word for word from a source. Direct quotations in college papers always require some form of documentation. Similarly, identify the sources for any diagrams, statistics, charts, or pictures. For detailed discussions, with examples, of the major documentation styles such as MLA, see Chapters 10–13.

Select direct quotations strategically.   Every quotation in a piece of writing should contribute something your own words cannot convey. Use quotations for these purposes.

- to focus on a well-stated key idea in a source
- to show what others think about a subject—experts or the general public
- to lend support to facts or concepts
- to add strength or character to your argument or report
- to clarify or emphasize a point

Introduce all direct and indirect quotations. Use a context or frame to introduce all borrowed material. Such frames can precede, follow, or interrupt the borrowed words or ideas. Adjust the frame to fit grammatically with the quotation, or, if necessary, select the quotation to fit the sentence.

FRAME PRECEDES BORROWED MATERIAL

In 1896, Woodrow Wilson, who would become Princeton's president in 1902, declared, "It is not learning but the spirit of service that will give a college a place in the public annals of the nation."
—Ernest L. Boyer

FRAME FOLLOWS BORROWED MATERIAL

"One reason you may have more colds if you hold back tears is that, when you're under stress, your body puts out steroids which affect your immune system and reduce your resistance to disease," **Dr. Broomfield comments.**
—Barbara Lang Stern

FRAME INTERRUPTS BORROWED MATERIAL

"Whatever happens," **he [Karl Marx] wrote grimly to Engels,** "I hope the bourgeoisie as long as they exist will have cause to remember my carbuncles."
—Paul Johnson

DESTINATION

For 150 verbs you can use in place of the verb *said* when quoting someone, visit Weber State University's Writing Center at <http://catsis.weber.edu/writingcenter/sentence.htm>. ■

Use brackets and ellipses (. . .) to show omissions. Only part of a long quotation may suit your essay; ellipses allow you to present only the appropriate portion. Ellipses show where you have omitted material. If you use ellipses, be sure the omission doesn't change the meaning of the original passage. MLA style requires brackets around ellipses in quoted material.

Although working with any part of an original scripture text is difficult, Barry Hoberman, author of "Translating the Bible," describes the text of the Old Testament as "**the stuff of scholarly nightmares.**" He explains that while "**the entire New Testament was written within fifty to a hundred years, the books of the Old Testament were composed and edited over a period of about a thousand. [. . .] The oldest portions of**

the Old Testament [. . .] are probably a group of poems that appear [. . .] to date from roughly the twelfth and eleventh centuries B.C."

Use [*sic*] to indicate an obvious error.   To show that you have copied a passage accurately—errors and all—place the expression *sic* in brackets one space after any mistake.

> Mr. Vincent's letter went on: "I would have preferred a younger bride, but I decided to marry the old window [*sic*] anyway."

Place short prose quotations between quotation marks.   Longer quotations should be indented. For guidelines by documentation style, see pages 63 (MLA) and 102 (APA).

DESTINATION

For help with using quotations in MLA style, consult "Big Dog's Quotation Mechanics Guide" at <http://gabiscott.com/pages/bigdog_mla_old.html>. ∎

d Document Sources Precisely

Documentation is the evidence you provide to support the ideas presented in a research project. Some writers do not realize that by documenting sources inadequately or carelessly, they can destroy the credibility of their research.

Representing the words or ideas you found in a source as your own constitutes plagiarism, a serious charge against any writer. Quite simply, you should respect and acknowledge the work you borrow from other writers or colleagues.

Chapters 10–13 present four systems for documenting sources: Modern Language Association (MLA), American Psychological Association (APA), Chicago Manual of Style (CMS), and Council of Biology Editors (CBE). Here we offer general guidelines for acknowledging and using sources.

Document information from sources fully.   Document all ideas, opinions, facts, and information that you acquire from sources and that cannot be considered common knowledge. Common knowledge includes the facts, dates, events, information, and concepts that can be looked up quickly in a standard reference book such as a dictionary or an encyclopedia.

For example, you can learn from an encyclopedia that the Battle of Waterloo was fought on June 18, 1815; thus you do not have to document it. You also need not document common knowledge within a field—what's generally agreed on by experts. But if your subject is controversial, you may want to document even facts or ideas considered common knowledge. Consider your audience: Nonspecialist readers may need more documentation than experts in your research area.

Provide dates for important events, major figures, and works of literature and art. Identify any people readers might not recognize.

After the great fire of London (1666), the city was . . .

Henry Highland Garnet (1815–82), American abolitionist and radical, . . .

Acknowledge all direct and indirect uses of anyone else's work.
If you decide to quote all or part of a selection, you must use quotation marks or indentation to indicate that you are borrowing the writer's exact words. In academic papers, you must also identify the author, work, publisher, date, and location of the passage through formal documentation, such as MLA or APA.

If you quote a source indirectly, borrowing the information but not the words, you must include a parenthetical note acknowledging the source of the information. For example, if you paraphrase or summarize a source, you must document this indirect borrowing. For MLA examples, see pages 60–63. For APA, see pages 99–102.

> E-Tips
>
> It is dangerously easy to plagiarize electronic sources inadvertently. Once a sentence or paragraph is in your file, it is extremely difficult to separate it from your own words. If you cut and paste a paragraph—even a sentence—be sure to document the source immediately in your notes.

Avoid plagiarism.
A proper summary or paraphrase of a source should be entirely in your own words. Some writers mistakenly believe that they can avoid a charge of plagiarism by rearranging or changing a few words in a selection; they are wrong.

Compare the plagiarized paraphrase and summary on page 58 with the acceptable versions on pages 53 and 54.

PLAGIARIZED PARAPHRASE

The catastrophe now unfolding aboard the *Mir* space station argues against launching people to Mars any time soon. To consider a manned Mars mission now is like planning your next airflight during a midair crisis.

The difficulty is sending people into outer space.

Most of the really useful things achieved in space have been done with automated spaceships controlled by technicians on Earth. The record is quite impressive—scientific probes to the planets and beyond, communications satellites, weather satellites, reconnaissance satellites, the global positioning system. . . .

PLAGIARIZED SUMMARY

Alex Roland, chair of history at Duke University and a former historian at NASA, argues in *USA Today* (7 July 1997) <u>that all the really useful things done in space have been achieved with automated spacecraft controlled by people on Earth. Machines can reach more places, stay longer, and take more risks than people.</u>

You'll see the faults very readily when you compare these plagiarized paragraphs with the opening paragraphs in Roland's original editorial on page 52.

You can appreciate how tempting it might be to slip these words into the body of a paper, forgetting that you didn't write them yourself. To avoid plagiarism, the safest practice is to *always* use your own words in paraphrases and summaries.

Links in hypertexts (such as World Wide Web pages) can function as a type of documentation: They can take readers directly to supporting material or sources. Use links judiciously—avoid too many on a page, and explain to your readers where a highlighted passage is leading them.

DESTINATION

For a comprehensive discussion about and examples of plagiarism, visit Student Judicial Services at the University of Texas at Austin at <http://www.utexas.edu/depts/dos/sjs/academicintegrity.html>. ■

Documentation

10 MLA Style

"Life itself is a quotation."
—JORGE LUIS BORGES, writer, poet

The Modern Language Association (MLA) style of documentation is used in many professional fields in the humanities. The basic procedures for using MLA style are spelled out in this chapter. For any problems not addressed here, consult the *MLA Handbook for Writers of Research Papers*, fifth edition, by Joseph Gibaldi. Style updates are also available at the MLA Web site at <http://www.mla.org>.

EXPRESS!

You need to take only two steps to use MLA style properly.

1. Create an in-text note for every source as you use it in a writing project.
2. Create an entry on a Works Cited page for each source you use.

Notice in the following example how the in-text note in parentheses tells readers to look for a work by Carter on the Works Cited page; they will find the quoted sentence on page 287 of Carter's book.

```
Many find modern society hectic and
overpowering: "we seem to spend all of our
time searching for bits of peace and quiet
for ourselves" (Carter 287).
```

Your readers can then turn to the Works Cited page for complete publication information about the source.

```
                Works Cited
Carter, Stephen L. Civility: Manners, Morals,
     and the Etiquette of Democracy. New
     York: HarperPerennial, 1998.
```

a In-Text Citations

The main purpose of the in-text citation is to direct your reader to the original source of the information you are citing. See Section 10c, MLA Models, for more than sixty examples of in-text notes and their corresponding Works Cited entries. For formatting of in-text notes, see "In-Text Citations: MLA Format," page 63.

1. A work that includes an author and page number

   Either enclose the author's last name and the relevant page number(s) within parentheses, or name the author of the source in the body of the text and place only the page number within the parentheses.

   ```
   Many find modern society hectic and
   overpowering: "[W]e seem to spend all of our
   time searching for bits of peace and quiet
   for ourselves" (Carter 287).
   ```

   ```
   Stephen L. Carter, professor of law at Yale,
   notes that "we seem to spend all of our time
   searching for bits of peace and quiet for
   ourselves" (287).
   ```

   Use the second form when you build an entire paragraph from material in a single source, or when you are citing a complete book, article, or Web site rather than just a specific chapter, section, or passage.

2. A work without conventional authors or page numbers

   Ordinarily, cite the source just by naming it or describing it within the body of the writing project itself.

   ```
   The Media Research Center Web site offers . . .
   ```

   ```
   The Arkansas State Highway Map indicates . . .
   ```

   ```
   Software such as Microsoft's FoxPro . . .
   ```

   If an electronic source includes paragraph numbers, screen numbers, or titles for the Web pages you are citing, you can put this helpful information in parentheses.

3. **A work without an author (but with page numbers)—for example, an unsigned article in a magazine or newspaper**

   List the title, shortened if necessary, and the page number. Shortened titles must always begin with the words used to alphabetize the entry on the Works Cited page.

   ```
   ("In the Thicket" 18)
   ```

   ```
                   Works Cited
   "In the Thicket of Things." Texas Monthly
        Apr. 1994: 18.
   ```

4. **More than one work by a single author**

   Place a comma after the author's last name and identify the particular work being cited, using a shortened title.

   ```
   (Altick, Victorian People 190-192)
   ```

   ```
   (Altick, Victorian Studies 59)
   ```

   ```
                   Works Cited
   Altick, Richard D. Victorian People and
        Ideas. New York: Norton, 1973.
   ---. Victorian Studies in Scarlet. New York:
        Norton, 1977.
   ```

5. **More than a single work in one note**

   Separate the citations with a semicolon.

   ```
   (Polukord 13-16; Ryan and Weber 126)
   ```

6. **Two or more sources in a single sentence**

   Place the parenthetical notes right after the specific statements they support.

   ```
   While the budget cuts might go deeper than
   originally reported (Kinsley 42), there is
   no reason to believe that "throwing more
   taxpayers' dollars into a bottomless pit"
   (Doggett 62) will do much to reform "one of
   the least productive job training programs
   ever devised by the federal government"
   (Will 28).
   ```

   Notice that all the parenthetical notes are placed *outside* the quotation marks.

7. **Author quoted by another source**

Include "qtd. in" ("quoted in") before the name of the source.

```
(qtd. in Cavin 195)
```

8. **Quotations of more than four typed lines**

Indent a long quotation ten spaces from the left margin, omit quotation marks, and place the parenthetical note outside the final punctuation mark.

```
Winner of the Nobel Peace Prize in 1950,
Ralph Bunche, who died in 1971, left an
enduring legacy:
```

> His memory lives on, especially in
> the long struggle for human
> dignity and against racial
> discrimination and bigotry, and in
> the growing effectiveness of the
> United Nations in resolving
> conflicts and keeping the peace.
> (Urquhart 458)

In-Text Citations: MLA Format

- A single typed space separates the author's name and the page number: (Carter 287)
- The note itself falls *outside* the quotation marks: ". . . ourselves" (Carter 287)
- The final punctuation for the sentence comes *after* the note: (Carter 287).*
- Page numbers are not preceded by *p.* or *pp.* or by a comma: (Bly 253-54)

*Exception: The one exception is a quotation longer than four typed lines. See #8, above.

---

b The Works Cited Page

On a separate page at the end of your project, list alphabetically every source you cited. Include only sources you actually mention in the body of the project, not all that you might have examined in preparing the work. Title the list "Works Cited."

Works Cited Page: MLA Style

- Center the title "Works Cited" at the top of the page, with no quotation marks.
- Arrange the items alphabetically by the last name of the author. If no author is given, list the work according to the first word of its title, excluding *The, A,* and *An.*
- The first line of each entry touches the left-hand margin. Subsequent lines of an entry are indented five spaces.
- Double-space the entire list. Do not quadruple-space between entries unless your instructor asks you to.
- Punctuate items carefully. Don't forget the period at the end of each entry.
- If you have two or more entries by the same author, use the author's name for the first entry only. For subsequent entries, use three hyphens followed by a period. List the titles in alphabetical order. For an example, see #4, page 62.
- Shorten publishers' names whenever possible. Drop words such as *Company, Inc., LTD, Bro.,* and *Books.* Abbreviate *University* to *U* and *University Press* to *UP.* For example: *Charles Scribner's Sons* becomes *Scribner's; University of Chicago Press* becomes *U of Chicago P.* See also #21 on page 71.

```
                        Works Cited
     Arni, Sherry. "I Can Live with It." English
          Journal 79 (Nov. 1990): 76.
     "Chapters 110 and 128, Subchapter C." Texas
          Education Agency Administrative Rules.
          1 Sept. 1998. Texas Education Agency. 6
          March 2000 <http://www.tea.state.tx.us/
          rules/tac/ch110_128c.html>.
     Corbett, H. Dickson, and Bruce L. Wilson.
          Testing, Reform, and Rebellion.
          Norwood: Ablex, 1991.
```

---

c   MLA Models

Below you will find MLA models to follow in creating in-text notes and the corresponding Works Cited entries for more than sixty kinds of sources. Simply locate the type of source you need to cite in the MLA Models Index and then locate that item by number in the list that follows.

MLA Models Index

(continued)

MLA Models Index (continued)

1. **Book, Generic—MLA**   Provide author, title, place of publication, publisher, and year of publication.

   Note: (Prosek 246-47)

                         Works Cited
   Prosek, James. The Complete Angler: A
         Connecticut Yankee Follows in the
         Footsteps of Walton. New York:
         HarperCollins, 1999.

2. **Book, Two or Three Authors or Editors—MLA**

   Note: (Collier and Horowitz 24)

                         Works Cited
   Collier, Peter, and David Horowitz.
         Destructive Generation: Second Thoughts
         About the '60s. New York: Summit, 1989.

3. **Book, Four or More Authors or Editors—MLA**   You have two options. You can name all the authors in both the parenthetical note and Works Cited entry.

   Note: (Guth, Rico, Ruszkiewicz, and Bridges 95)

                         Works Cited
   Guth, Hans P., Gabriele L. Rico, John
         Ruszkiewicz, and Bill Bridges. The
         Rhetoric of Laughter: The Best and Worst
         of Humor Night. Fort Worth: Harcourt,
         1996.

Alternatively, you can name just the first author given on the title page and use the Latin abbreviation *et al.,* which means "and others."

Note: (Guth et al. 95)

Works Cited

Guth, Hans P., et al. The Rhetoric of
    Laughter: The Best and Worst of Humor
    Night. Fort Worth: Harcourt, 1996.

4. **Book, Revised by a Second Author—MLA** Sometimes you may need to cite a book by its original author, even when it has been revised. In such a case, place the editor's name after the title of the book.

Note: (Guerber 20)

Works Cited

Guerber, Hélène Adeline. The Myths of Greece
    and Rome. Ed. Dorothy Margaret Stuart.
    3rd ed. London: Harrap, 1965.

5. **Book, Edited—Focus on the Original Author—MLA**

Note: (Cor. 3.3.119-35)

Works Cited

Shakespeare, William. The Tragedy of
    Coriolanus. Ed. Reuben Brower. New York:
    Signet, 1966.

Coriolanus is a play by Shakespeare, so the note provides act, scene, and line numbers—not author and page numbers.

6. **Book, Edited—Focus on the Editor—MLA**

Note: (Brower xxiii-1)

Works Cited

Brower, Reuben, ed. The Tragedy of
    Coriolanus. By William Shakespeare. New
    York: Signet, 1966.

7. **Book, Edited—Focus on the Editor, More Than One Editor—MLA**

Note: (Kittredge and Smith xvi-xvii)

Works Cited

Kittredge, William, and Annick Smith, eds.
The Last Best Place: A Montana
Anthology. Seattle: U of Washington P,
1988.

8. **Book, Written by a Group—MLA**

Note: The Reader's Digest Fix-It-Yourself
Manual explains the importance of a UL label
(123).

Works Cited

Reader's Digest. Fix-It-Yourself Manual.
Pleasantville: Reader's Digest, 1977.

9. **Book with No Author—MLA** List the book by its title
excluding *The, A,* or *An.*

Note: (Kodak 56-58)
Note: The Kodak Guide to 35mm Photography
lists color film types in a useful chart
(56-58).

Works Cited

Kodak Guide to 35mm Photography. 6th ed.
Rochester: Eastman, 1989.

10. **Book, Focus on a Foreword, Introduction, Preface, or Afterword—MLA**

Note: (O'Rourke 5)

Works Cited

O'Rourke, P. J. Introduction. Road Trips,
Head Trips, and Other Car-Crazed
Writings. Ed. by Jean Lindamood. New
York: Atlantic, 1996. 1-8.

11. **Work of More Than One Volume—MLA** When you use
only one volume of a multivolume set, identify both the volume you have used and the total number of volumes in the set.

Note: (Spindler 17-18)

```
              Works Cited
Spindler, Karlheinz. Abstract Algebra with
     Applications. Vol. 1. New York: Dekker,
     1994. 2 vols.
```

If you use more than one volume of a set, identify the specific volumes in the parenthetical notes as you cite them. Then, in the Works Cited entry, list the total number of volumes in that set.

Notes: (Spindler 1: 17-18); (Spindler 2: 369)

```
              Works Cited
Spindler, Karlheinz. Abstract Algebra with
     Applications. 2 vols. New York: Dekker,
     1994.
```

12. **Book, Translation—Focus on the Original Author—MLA**

Note: (Freire 137-38)

```
              Works Cited
Freire, Paulo. Learning to Question: A
     Pedagogy of Liberation. Trans. Tony
     Coates. New York: Continuum, 1989.
```

13. **Book, Translation—Focus on the Translator—MLA**

Note: (Swanton 17-18)

```
              Works Cited
Swanton, Michael, trans. Beowulf. New York:
     Barnes, 1978.
```

14. **Book in a Foreign Language—MLA**

Note: (Bablet and Jacquot 59)

```
              Works Cited
Bablet, Denis, and Jean Jacquot. Les Voies de
     la création théâtrale. Paris: Editions
     du Centre National de la Recherche
     Scientifique, 1977.
```

15. **Book, Republished—MLA** Give original publication dates for works of fiction that have been through many editions and reprints.

Note: (Herbert 146)

Works Cited

Herbert, Frank. <u>Dune</u>. 1965. New York:
Berkeley, 1977.

16. **Book, Part of a Series—MLA** Give the series name just
before the place of publication.

Note: (Pemberton xii)

Works Cited

Pemberton, Michael, ed. <u>The Ethics of Writing</u>
<u>Instruction: Issues in Theory and</u>
<u>Practice</u>. Perspectives on Writing:
Theory, Research, Practice 4. Stamford:
Ablex, 2000.

17. **Book, a Reader or Anthology—MLA** When you quote
from the front matter of the collection, the page numbers
may sometimes be Roman numerals. (To cite a selection
from within an anthology, see model 29.)

Note: (Lunsford and Ruszkiewicz xxi-xxvi)

Works Cited

Lunsford, Andrea A., and John J. Ruszkiewicz,
eds. <u>The Presence of Others: Voices and</u>
<u>Images That Call for Response</u>. 3rd ed.
New York: Bedford, 2000.

18. **Book, a Second, Third, or Later Edition—MLA**

Note: (Rombauer 480-81)

Works Cited

Rombauer, Marjorie Dick. <u>Legal Problem</u>
<u>Solving: Analysis, Research, and</u>
<u>Writing</u>. 5th ed. St. Paul: West, 1991.

19. **Chapter in a Book—MLA**

Note: (Shalit 144-60)

Works Cited

Shalit, Wendy. "Male Character." A Return to
    Modesty: Discovering the Lost Virtue.
    New York: Free, 1999. 144-60.

20. **Book Published Before 1900—MLA** Omit the name of
    the publisher in citations to works published prior to 1900.

Note: (Bowdler 2: 47)

Works Cited

Bowdler, Thomas, ed. The Family Shakespeare.
    10 vols. London, 1818.

21. **Book Issued by a Division of a Publisher—a Special Im-
    print—MLA** Attach the special imprint (Vintage in this
    case) to the publisher's name with a hyphen.

Note: (Hofstader 192-93)

Works Cited

Hofstader, Douglas. Gödel, Escher, Bach:
    An Eternal Golden Braid. New York:
    Vintage-Random, 1980.

22. **Dissertation or Thesis—Published—MLA** If published
    by University Microfilms International (UMI), provide the
    order number as the last item.

Note: (Rifkin 234)

Works Cited

Rifkin, Myra Lee. Burial, Funeral and
    Mourning Customs in England, 1558-1662.
    Diss. Bryn Mawr, 1977. Ann Arbor: UMI,
    1977. DDJ78-01385.

23. **Dissertation or Thesis—Unpublished—MLA** The title
    appears between quotation marks.

Note: (Altman 150)

Works Cited

Altman, Jack, Jr. "The Politics of Health
    Planning and Regulation." Diss.

> Massachusetts Institute of Technology,
> 1983.

24. **Book Review/Movie Review—Titled or Untitled—MLA**
Not all reviews have titles, so the form for a review may vary slightly.

Note: (Keen 39)

Works Cited

Keen, Maurice. "The Knight of Knights." Rev.
> of <u>William Marshall: The Flower of
> Chivalry</u>, by Georges Duby. <u>New York
> Review of Books</u> 16 Jan. 1986: 39–40.

Notice that a book title (*Uncle Tom's Cabin*) within a book title is not underscored or italicized (Uncle Tom's Cabin *and American Culture*).

Note: (Baym 691-92)

Works Cited

Baym, Nina. Rev. of Uncle Tom's Cabin <u>and
> American Culture</u>, by Thomas F. Gossett.
> <u>Journal of American History</u> 72 (1985):
> 691–92.

Here's the form for a film review found online, in this case in the e-zine *Slate*. The citation includes the date of the review itself and the date it was accessed online.

Note: David Edelstein finds Ben Affleck an
> unlikely convict in <u>Reindeer Games</u> . . .

Works Cited

Edelstein, David. "Parlor Games." Rev. of
> <u>Reindeer Games</u>, dir. John Frankenheimer.
> <u>Slate</u> 25 Feb. 2000. 8 Mar 2000 <http://
> slate.msn.com/Movie Review/00-02-25/
> MovieReview.asp>.

25. **Article in a Scholarly Journal—MLA**   Scholarly journals are usually identified by volume number or season. Such journals are usually paginated year by year, with a year's work treated as one volume. Provide author, title of article, title of journal, volume number, date of publication, and page numbers.

Note: (Smith 301)

Works Cited

Smith, Laurajane. "Heritage Management as
     Postprocessual Archaeology?" <u>Antiquity</u>
     64 (June 1994): 300-09.

If a scholarly journal is paginated issue by issue, place a period and an issue number after the volume number.

Note: (Morgenroth 91-92)

Works Cited

Morgenroth, Joyce. "Dressing for the Dance"
     <u>Wilson Quarterly</u> 22.2 (Spring 1998):
     88-95.

26. **Article in a Popular Magazine—MLA** Magazines are paginated issue by issue and identified by the seasonal, monthly, or weekly date of publication. Provide author, title of article, title of magazine, date of publication, and page numbers.

Note: (Murray 63)

Works Cited

Murray, Spencer. "Roaming Wyoming." <u>Open Road</u>
     Spring 1999: 60-65.

Articles in magazines often don't appear on consecutive pages. When that's the case, list the relevant page number(s) in the parenthetical note. In the Works Cited entry give the first page on which it appears, followed by a plus sign—for example, *112+*.

Note: (Mackay 170)

Works Cited

Mackay, Jordan. "A Murder on Campus." <u>Texas
     Monthly</u> Jan. 2000: 112+.

27. **Article in a Weekly or Biweekly Magazine—MLA**

Note: (Smolowe 20)

Works Cited

Smolowe, Jill. "When Violence Hits Home."
     <u>Time</u> 18 July 1994: 18-25.

28. Article in a Monthly Magazine—MLA

Note: (Bond 90)

Works Cited

Bond, Constance. "If You Can't Bear to Part
     with It, Open a New Museum." <u>Smithsonian</u>
     Apr. 1995: 90-97.

29. Article or Selection from a Reader or Anthology—MLA
List the item on the Works Cited page by the author of the
piece you are actually citing, not the editor(s) of the collection.

Note: (King 417-20)

Works Cited

King, Robert. "Should English Be the Law?"
     <u>The Presence of Others: Voices and
     Images That Call for Response</u>. 3rd ed.
     Ed. Andrea Lunsford and John
     Ruszkiewicz. New York: Bedford, 2000.
     409-21.

When you cite two or more selections from a reader or an
anthology, list that collection fully on the Works Cited page.

Lunsford, Andrea, and John Ruszkiewicz, eds.
     <u>The Presence of Others: Voices and
     Images That Call for Response</u>. 3rd ed.
     New York: Bedford, 2000.

Then, still in the Works Cited list, identify the authors and
titles of all articles you cite from that reader or anthology,
followed by the name of the editors and page numbers of
those selections.

Note: (King 417-20)
Note: (Turkle 453)

Works Cited

King, Robert. "Should English Be the Law?"
     Lunsford and Ruszkiewicz 409-21.
Turkle, Shirley. "Who Am We?" Lunsford and
     Ruszkiewicz 442-58.

30. **Article in a Newspaper—MLA** The plus sign indicates that an article continues beyond the designated page, but not necessarily on consecutive pages.

Note: (Peterson 2A)

                    Works Cited
Peterson, Karen S. "Turns Out We Are
        'Sexually Conventional.'" USA Today 7
        Oct. 1994: 1A+.

31. **Editorial in a Newspaper—Author Not Named—MLA**

Note: ("Negro College" 28)

                    Works Cited
"Negro College Fund: Mission Is Still
        Important on 50th Anniversary."
        Editorial. Dallas Morning News 8 Oct.
        1994: A28.

32. **Letter to the Editor—MLA**

Note: (Cantu 4)

                    Works Cited
Cantu, Tony. Letter. San Antonio Light 14
        Jan. 1986, southwest ed.: C4.

33. **Cartoon—MLA** Describe a cartoon in the text of your essay.

Note: In the cartoon "Squib" by Miles
Mathis . . .

                    Works Cited
Mathis, Miles. "Squib." Cartoon. Daily Texan
        15 Jan. 1986: 19.

34. **Reference Work or Encyclopedia (Familiar or Online)—MLA** Identify the edition you are using by its date. Omit the names of editors and most publishing information. No page number is given in the parenthetical note when a work is arranged alphabetically.

Note: (Benedict)

Works Cited

Benedict, Roger William. "Northwest Passage."
    Encyclopaedia Britannica: Macropaedia.
    1974 ed.

A citation for an online encyclopedia article would include a date of access and electronic address. However, the online version might not list an author.

Works Cited

"Northwest Passage." Britannica Online.
    Encyclopaedia Britannica. 8 Feb. 2000
    <http://search.eb.com/bol/
    topic?eu=57696&sctn=1>.

35. **Reference Work (Specialized or Less Familiar)—MLA** With less familiar reference tools, a full entry is required. (See #34 for a comparison with familiar reference works.)

Note: (Kovesi)

Works Cited

Kovesi, Julius. "Hungarian Philosophy." The
    Encyclopedia of Philosophy. Ed. Paul
    Edwards. 8 vols. New York: Macmillan,
    1967.

36. **Bulletin or Pamphlet—MLA**

Note: (Morgan 8-9)

Works Cited

Morgan, Martha G., ed. Campus Guide to
    Computer & Web Services. Austin: U of
    Texas, 1999.

37. **Government Document—MLA** Give the name of the government (national, state, or local) and the agency issuing the report, the title of the document, and publishing information. If it is a congressional document other than the *Congressional Record,* identify the Congress and, when important, the session (for example, *99th Cong., 1st sess.*) after the title of the document.

Note: This information is from the 1985-86
Official Congressional Directory (182-84).

```
                Works Cited
United States. Cong. Joint Committee on
     Printing. 1985-86 Official Congressional
     Directory. 99th Cong., 1st sess.
     Washington: GPO, 1985.
```

To cite the *Congressional Record*, give only the date and page number.

```
Cong. Rec. 8 Feb. 1974: 3942-43.
```

38. **Computer Software—MLA**   Give the author if known, the version number if any (for example: *Microsoft Word*. Vers. 7.0), the manufacturer, the date, and (optionally) the system needed to run it. Name the software in your text.

Note: With software such as Connectix's
Virtual PC . . .

```
                Works Cited
Virtual PC. Vers. 3.0. San Mateo: Connectix,
     1999.
```

39. **WWW Page—Generic—MLA**   A typical MLA Works Cited entry for an electronic source may include the following information, though few items will require all these elements:

- the creator or author of the site, if any
- the title of the complete electronic site, underlined (the title of an individual page might appear between quotation marks)
- the editor (if any) of the electronic site, database, or text, with role indicated (for example, *Ed.*)
- the version (if any) of the source
- the date of electronic publication or most recent update
- the identity of the institution or group (if any) sponsoring the electronic site
- the date you accessed the information
- the electronic address between angle brackets < >, followed by a period.

Here, for example, is a citation to an entire Web site.

Note: More information on National Parks in
the United States can be found at Parknet.

```
                Works Cited
Parknet. National Park Service. 12 Dec. 1999
     <http://www.nps.gov/>.
```

A citation to a particular page on that Web site would look like the following.

Note: ("New Lease")

Works Cited

"A New Lease on Life: Museum Conservation
in the National Park Service." Parknet.
7 Dec. 1999. National Park Service. 10
Feb. 2000 <http://www.cr.nps.gov/csd/
exhibits/conservation/>.

E-Tips

Since most Web sites and other online sources do not
have page numbers, avoid in-text parenthetical citations
by identifying the site in the body of the paper.

40. **WWW—Online Book—MLA**   If available, give an original date of publication, the date of the electronic source, and the date you accessed the information.

Note: In the online version of Henry Adams's
The Education of Henry Adams . . .

Works Cited

Adams, Henry. The Education of Henry Adams:
An Autobiography. Boston: Houghton, 1918.
The American Studies Group at UVA
Hypertext. 1996. The University of
Virginia. 6 Mar. 1998 <http://
xroads.virginia.edu/~HYPER/hadams/
hahome.html>.

41. **WWW—Online Scholarly Journal—MLA**

Note: In "Tenure and Technology," Katz,
Walker, and Cross argue . . .

Works Cited

Katz, Seth, Janice Walker, and Janet Cross.
"Tenure and Technology: New Values, New
Guidelines." Kairos 2.1 (1997). 20 July
1997 <http://english.ttu.edu/kairos/
2.1/coverweb/bridge.html>.

42. **WWW—Online Popular Magazine—MLA**

Note: Shafer claims in "The New Walter
Cronkite" that . . .

Works Cited

Shafer, Jack. "The New Walter Cronkite."
    Slate 18 Oct. 1996. 12 July 1997
    <http://slate.msn.com/Assessment/
    96-10-18/Assessment.asp>.

43. **WWW—Online News Source or Newspaper—MLA**

Note: Sue Ann Pressley suggests that the
movement to teach manners in school
is . . .

Works Cited

Pressley, Sue Ann. "Louisiana's Courtesy
    Call." The Washington Post Online
    5 Mar. 2000. 6 Mar. 2000 <http://
    www.washingtonpost.com/wpdyn/articles/
    A11177-2000Mar4.html>.

Here's how to cite an online editorial. In this case, the date of
the editorial and the date of access to it are the same.

Note: In an editorial on 13 July 1997, the New
York Times . . .

Works Cited

"The Proved and the Unproved." Editorial. New
    York Times on the Web 13 July 1997. 13
    July 1997 <http://www.nytimes.com/yr/mo/
    day/editorial/13sunl.html>.

44. **WWW—Personal Home Page—MLA**

Note: For an example of a digitally enhanced
photograph, see the home page of Brett R.
Elliott.

Works Cited

Elliott, Brett R. Home page. 4 Nov. 1998. 5
    Mar. 2000. <http://www.cwrl.utexas.edu/
    wcb/students/belliot5/belliot5.html>.

45. **Listserv/Newsgroup/Usenet Newsgroup—MLA** Identify the author of the document or posting; put the subject line of the posting between quotation marks, followed by the words *Online posting* and the date on which the item was originally posted; give the name of the listserv, followed by the date you accessed the item, and the electronic address in the angle brackets.

    Note: Christy Heady recommends . . .

    Works Cited

    Heady, Christy. "Buy or Lease? Depends on How
        Long You'll Keep the Car." Online
        posting. 7 July 1997. ClariNet. 14 July
        1997 <news:clari.biz.industry.automotive>.

    Sometimes the name on a listserv may be incomplete or unconventional, but reproduce it just as it appears.

46. **Synchronous Communication (MOOs, MUDs)—MLA** Provide the speaker and/or site, the title of the session or event, the date of the session, the forum for the communication (if specified), the date of access, and the electronic address.

    Note: In LinguaMOO, Inept_Guest observes . . .

    Works Cited

    Inept_Guest. Discussion of disciplinary
        politics in rhet/comp. 12 Mar. 1998.
        LinguaMOO. 12 Mar. 1998
        <telnet:lingua.utdallas.edu 8888>.

47. **Email—MLA**

    Note: Pacheco makes the case that Al Gore . . .

    Works Cited

    Pacheco, Miguel. "Re: Gore or Bush?" E-mail
        to the author. 1 Nov. 2000.

48. **CD-ROM/Diskette Database or Publication—MLA** To cite a CD-ROM or similar electronic database, provide basic information about the source itself—author, title, and publication information. Identify the publication medium (*CD-*

ROM; Diskette; Magnetic tape) and the name of the vendor if available. (The vendor is the company publishing or distributing the database.) Conclude with the date of electronic publication.

Note: (Bevington 98)

Works Cited

Bevington, David. "Castles in the Air: The
    Morality Plays." The Theater of Medieval
    Europe: New Research in Early Drama. Ed.
    Simon Eckchard. Cambridge: Cambridge UP,
    1993. MLA Bibliography. CD-ROM.
    SilverPlatter. Feb. 1995.

For a CD-ROM database that is often updated (*ProQuest*, for example), you must provide publication dates for the item you are examining and for the data disk itself.

Note: (Alva 407-10)

Works Cited

Alva, Sylvia Alatore. "Differential Patterns
    of Achievement Among Asian-American
    Adolescents." Journal of Youth and
    Adolescence 22 (1993): 407-23. Proquest
    General Periodicals. CD-ROM. UMI-
    Proquest. June 1994.

Cite a book, encyclopedia, play, or other item published on CD-ROM or diskette just as if it were a printed source, adding the medium of publication (*Diskette* or *CD-ROM*, for example). When page numbers aren't available, use the author's name in the text of the paper to avoid parenthetical citation.

Note: Bolter argues . . .

Works Cited

Bolter, Jay David. Writing Space: A Hypertext.
    Diskette. Hillsdale: Erlbaum, 1990.

49. Microfilm or Microfiche—MLA

Note: ("How Long?" 434)

Works Cited

"How Long Will the Chemise Last?" <u>Consumer
     Reports</u>. Aug. 1958: 434-37.

50. **Biblical Citation—MLA**   Titles of sacred works, including
    all versions of the Bible, are not underlined.

Note: (John 18:37-38)

Works Cited

The Jerusalem Bible. Ed. Alexander Jones.
     Garden City: Doubleday, 1966.

51. **Videotape/DVD—MLA**   Cite a video entry by title in most
    cases. You may include information about the producer, de-
    signer, performers, and so on. Identify the distributor, and
    provide a date.

Note: <u>Tae-Bo Workout</u> offers . . .

Works Cited

<u>Tao-Bo Workout: Instructional and Basic</u>.
     Perf. Billy Blanks. Videocassettes.
     Ventura, 1998.

Note: <u>The Matrix</u> DVD includes production notes
that . . .

Works Cited

<u>The Matrix (Widescreen edition)</u>. Perf. Keanu
     Reeves and Laurence Fishburne. DVD.
     Warner, 1999.

52. **Movie—MLA**   In most cases, list a movie by its title. Provide
    information about actors, producers, and so on, to suit your
    readers. Identify the distributor, and give a date of production.

Note: In Lucas's film <u>American Graffiti</u> . . .

Works Cited

<u>American Graffiti</u>. Dir. George Lucas. Perf.
     Richard Dreyfuss and Ronny Howard.
     Universal, 1973.

53. Television Program—MLA

Note: In the episode "No Surrender, No
Retreat" . . .

Works Cited

"No Surrender, No Retreat." Dir. Mike Vejar.
    Writ. Michael Straczynski. Perf. Bruce
    Boxleitner, Claudia Christian, and Mira
    Furlan. Babylon 5 KEYE-42, Austin. 28
    July 1997.

54. Radio Program—MLA

Note: Early episodes of Death Valley Days . . .

Works Cited

Death Valley Days. Created by Ruth Cornwall
    Woodman. NBC Radio. WNBC, New York. 30
    Sept. 1930.

55. Personal Interview—MLA

Note: In an interview, Rev. Peter Gomes
explains . . .

Works Cited

Gomes, Rev. Peter. Personal interview. 23
    Apr. 1997.

56. Musical Composition—MLA   List the work on the Works
Cited page by the name of the composer. If you have sheet
music or a score, give complete publication information. If
you don't have a score or sheet music, provide a simpler entry.

Note: Scott Joplin published "The Strenuous
Life" at a time . . .

Works Cited

Joplin, Scott. "The Strenuous Life: A Ragtime
    Two Step." St. Louis: Stark, 1902.

Note: Another Cole Porter song, "Too Darn
Hot" . . .

Works Cited

Porter, Cole. "Too Darn Hot." 1949.

57. **Recording/Audio Clip—MLA**

Note: An album such as <u>One Endless Night</u> by
Jimmie Dale Gilmore is a good example of . . .

Works Cited

Gilmore, Jimmie Dale. <u>One Endless Night</u>.
    Windchanger/Rounder, 2000.

Here is how to cite an audio clip from a Web site.

Note: The theme for NPR's <u>Car Talk</u>, "Dawgy
Mountain Breakdown" by David Grisman, is . . .

Works Cited

Grisman, David. "Dawgy Mountain Breakdown."
    <u>CarTalk at Cars.com</u>. Natl. Public
    Radio. 1990. 28 Feb. 2000 <http://
    cartalk.cars.com/Radio/Misc/Audio/RA/
    theme2.ram>.

58. **Speech—MLA**   If you have no printed text of the speech,
give the location and date of the address.

Note: Reagan explained his position in an
address to . . .

Works Cited

Reagan, Ronald. "The Geneva Summit Meeting: A
    Measure of Progress." U.S. Congress.
    Washington. 21 Nov. 1985.

With a printed text, give complete publication information.

Note: (O'Rourke 20)

Works Cited

O'Rourke, P. J. "Brickbats and Broomsticks."
    Capital Hilton. Washington. 2 Dec. 1992.
    Rpt. <u>American Spectator</u> Feb. 1993:
    20-21.

59. Lecture—MLA

Note: Addressing a conference of educators in
Cincinnati, William W. Cook . . .

Works Cited

Cook, William W. "Writing in the Spaces
    Left." Chair's Address. Conf. on Coll.
    Composition and Communication.
    Cincinnati. 19 Mar. 1992.

60. Advertisement—MLA

Note: An advertisement for the Subaru Outback
sedan includes . . .

Works Cited

Subaru Outback. Advertisement. Brill's
    Content Feb. 2000: 37.

List an online advertisement similarly. Provide an electronic
address and date of access.

Note: An Ameritrade Anniversary Offer
displays . . .

Works Cited

Ameritrade Anniversary Offer. Advertisement.
    15 Mar. 2000. <http://www.ameritrade.com/
    o.cgi?a=gby&o=rfg&p=/html/a.fhtml>.

61. Letter—Published—MLA

Note: (Eliot 427)

Works Cited

Eliot, George. "To Thomas Clifford Allbutt."
    1 Nov. 1873. In Selections from George
    Eliot's Letters. Ed. Gordon S. Haight.
    New Haven: Yale UP, 1985. 427.

62. Letter—Unpublished—MLA

Note: In a letter to Agnes Weinstein dated 23
May 1917, Albert Newton complains . . .

Works Cited

Newton, Albert. Letter to Agnes Weinstein. 23
    May 1917. Albert Newton Papers. Woodhill
    Lib., Cleveland.

63. Artwork/Photograph—MLA

Note: The work resembles both the painting
Ariel by Fuseli at the Folger and . . .

Works Cited

Fuseli, Henry. Ariel. Folger Shakespeare
    Lib., Washington, D.C.

64. Drama or Play—MLA For printed texts, provide the
usual Works Cited information. In parenthetical notes, give
the act, scene, and line numbers when the work is so divided;
give page numbers if it is not.

Note: (Ham. 5.2.219-24)

Works Cited

Shakespeare, William. The Tragedy of Hamlet,
    Prince of Denmark. Ed. Frank Kermode.
    The Riverside Shakespeare. 2nd ed.
    Ed. G. Blakemore Evans and J. J. M.
    Tobin. Boston: Houghton, 1997.
    1183-1245.

Note: (Stoppard 11-15)

Works Cited

Stoppard, Tom. Rosencrantz and Guildenstern
    Are Dead. New York: Grove, 1967.

For performances of plays, give the title, the author, and
then any specific information that seems relevant—director, performers, producers, set designer, theater company,
and so on. Conclude the entry with a theater, location, and
date.

Note: In a rare and memorable performance of
Shakespeare's Timon of Athens . . .

Works Cited

<u>Timon of Athens</u>. By William Shakespeare. Dir.
Michael Benthall. Perf. Ralph
Richardson, Paul Curran, and Margaret
Whiting. Old Vic, London. 5 Sept. 1956.

d Sample MLA Paper

MLA does not require a separate cover sheet or title page. If your instructor expects one, center the title of your paper and your name in the upper third of the sheet. Center the course title, your instructor's name, and the date of submission in the lower third of the sheet, double-spacing between the elements.

The first page of a paper without a separate title page will look like the sample on page 88. Check the following items when preparing your project.

- Number each page in the upper right-hand corner, one-half inch from the top, one inch from the right margin. Precede the page number with your last name.
- On the first page, place your name, your instructor's name, the course title, and the date in the upper left-hand corner, beginning one inch from the top of the page. Double space these items.
- Center the title a double space under the date. Capitalize the first and last word of the title. Capitalize all other words *except* articles (*a, an, the*), prepositions, the *to* in infinitives, and coordinating conjunctions—unless they are the first or last words.
- Do not underline or boldface the title. Do not use all caps, place the title between quotation marks, or end it with a period. Titles may, however, end with question marks or include words or phrases that are italicized, underlined, or between quotation marks.

  RIGHT Violence in Shakespeare's *Macbeth*

  RIGHT Dylan's "Like a Rolling Stone" Revisited

- Begin the body of the essay a double space below the title. Double-space the entire paper, including quotations.
- Use one-inch margins at the sides and bottom of each page.

General formatting guidelines for MLA in-text citations are given on page 63, and for the Works Cited list, on page 64.

Ben H. Brenneman

Professor Ruszkiewicz

Rhetoric 306

2 March 2000

Can Quality Survive the Standardized Test?

¶1   In Seeking Diversity, a book on teaching
middle school language arts, author and teacher
Linda Rief says, "I expect good reading and
writing, in which process and product are woven
tightly into literate tapestries of wonder and
awe" (10). Rief thus describes the Holy Grail of
writing instruction: a classroom in which students
learn to write because they care about the final
product and want to do excellent work. Such an
environment would teach students the ability to
write by turning them into writers. Unfortunately,
the American education system today is failing to
teach many students even the basic skills they
will need to survive. Statements by teachers that
"the greater number of the young people we teach
[. . .] do not know how to read, spell, write, use
correct grammar, do simple math, remember, use
logic" are supported by statistics showing that
"only 55% of the nation's 17-year-olds and 49% of
out-of-school adults are able to write an
acceptable letter ordering a product by mail"
(Neill 18). Yet the dominant response to this
problem--competency testing in our public schools--
may be destroying any regard students may have for
language by turning writing into a formulaic
exercise.

¶2   Many states, in fact, have already responded
to problems in their educational systems by
passing laws mandating the skills that students

must learn by a specified grade. The students'
ability to reach the objectives and the faculty's
ability to teach this "standards-based
curriculum" are then measured by statewide
standardized tests. Students and schools that
fall short of the mark can then be identified for
improvement. As Neill explains, "the strongest
argument in support of competency requirements is
the potential for motivating students, schools,
and districts" (8). The results of testing are
carefully monitored and publicized to show
continuing improvement in the performance of
public schools (see Table 1).

Table 1

Percentage of Students Passing All Texas
  Assessment of Academic Skills Exams (TAAS)

	1994	1995	1996	1997	1998	4 Yr. Gain
Grade 3	58	66	70	74	76	18
Grade 4	54	64	67	72	78	24
Grade 5	58	66	73	79	83	25
Grade 6	56	60	69	77	79	23
Grade 7	55	58	67	75	78	23
Grade 8	49	50	59	67	72	23
Grade 10	52	54	60	68	72	20

Source: Texas Business and Education Coalition.
  School Gains. 1999. 27 Feb. 2000. <http://
  www.tbec.org/gains.HTML>.

¶3   In many states this progress has been
motivated by attaching increasingly serious
consequences to the results of these tests.
Students who fail the state aptitude test may be
held back a grade, or they may even be denied a

high school diploma. Teachers are also under increasing pressure to get test scores up. Jack Kaufhold, a professor of educational psychology, notes that principals have been warned, "If your test scores don't go up, you may lose your job." He adds, "Teachers also know that if their students' achievement test scores fluctuate too much from year to year, they too could be demoted or dismissed" (14).

¶4   State officials justify these types of high-stakes assessment on the grounds that the skills the tests focus on are those students will need to function in society. They argue, moreover, that students who receive a quality education should have little trouble fulfilling the minimum requirements. For instance, the standards for writing set in Texas, called the "Texas Essential Knowledge and Skills" or TEKS, state that students who graduate high school must "write in a variety of forms using effective word choice, structure, and sentences with an emphasis on organizing logical arguments [. . .]; write in a voice and style appropriate to audience and purpose; and organize in writing to ensure coherence" ("Chapters"). In other words, everyone who receives a high school diploma should be able to communicate effectively in writing. Students demonstrate their skill during the Texas Assessment of Academic Skills (TAAS), by composing an essay. As Mary argues, on a WWW forum sponsored by Teachers.Net, "The TEKS based TAAS are a reflection of the specific standards the children of our state should meet. That's precisely what we should be teaching." Many teachers, however, find that their curriculums are already adequate. Their response to these requirements is like Sheri Arni's: "My answer has been to leave unchanged most of what happens in my classroom" (76). Rief, for example, gives her students "a two-day crash course [. . .] just before they take the state-mandated achievement tests [. . .]. Two days is all I allow" (180).

¶5   Unfortunately some schools fall short of the mark. The administrators in these institutions are then forced to make changes to the curriculum in order to raise scores quickly. In Maryland teachers responded to a writing test that they felt was too difficult by creating writing labs, increasing the amount of writing done in regular English, and cooperating between departments to focus on writing in all disciplines (Corbett and Wilson). This is the type of reform the tests were intended to produce. The instructors at this school improved their curriculum by finding innovative ways to teach their students how to write. Anne Shaughnessy, when preparing her students for the Florida assessment, had them discuss their responses to a sample prompt. She showed them that the qualities they felt made an essay successful were the same criteria that would be used to score their tests. She then had them use the actual rubric to score their essays in class. In this way Shaughnessy gave her students some insight into the logic behind the test, making it more than simply an arbitrary exercise. She writes, "Clearly I was teaching to the test, but I was also introducing activities that extended rather than displaced the writing curriculum" (56).

¶6   These improvements are certainly commendable. They occur when schools are blessed with creative teachers who are willing to take risks. However, many educators, when faced with the possibility of unemployment, turn to the tried-and-true method the army uses to train new recruits: drill, drill, drill. In the Maryland case, for example, Corbett and Wilson note that "teachers would stop what they were doing with students [. . .] and inject an intense period of [. . .] 'drill and review' specifically related to the test" (124). When preparing for a writing exam, students spend this period responding to practice prompts, often from previous tests that have been released by the state. A teacher in Texas reported that she "had to give a writing test AND a reading test every six weeks" (Melissa). In teaching circles this strategy is known as the "drill-and-kill" approach. In other words, students are drilled until all genuine interest in the subject is killed by weeks of prompt writing.

¶7   Teachers are alarmed by the drill-and-kill approach to test preparation. They fear that the focus of their instruction has shifted from producing excellent writing for a general audience to producing adequate writing in order to avoid the wrath of the state. This attitude is communicated to the students simply by the time spent in practice. As one Texan teacher laments, "from mid-January through April we are not teachers, we are masters of how to take a test" (Linda/tx). In this environment students begin to believe that mastery of the test is the goal of their education. They often create, or are even taught, ways to improve their scores by manipulating the test. According to Donna Garner, any student who got a high score on the essay portion of the TAAS could miss most of the questions on the grammar-oriented part of the test and still pass. She says that, when students understand this, "it's rather hard to get them to see the seriousness of correct grammar, spelling, punctuation, capitalization, and sentence structure. Once the students learn to 'play the TAAS game' by scripting their essays to a set pattern, the accuracy of the content is of little importance to them." These students see writing as a task they will have to perform once in order to graduate, not as a skill they will need to communicate effectively in the real world.

¶8   Kaufhold descries this mindset as "convergent thinking." He says that these types of tests emphasize "the need to search for one right answer. Creative ideas or divergent thinking is discouraged as students narrow the scope of their thinking toward what will be on the test" (14). Ironically, such narrowing is actually endorsed by A. D. Rison in his 1990 book designed to help students pass the language arts portion of the TAAS. He supports the use of a "Rison Design," basically the typical hourglass shape long used to teach the five-paragraph theme. He believes that students should use this design so that "many competing functions, thinking, writing, vision, and other unnecessary movements are lessened" (136). And yet for years, many teachers of composition have complained that

Brenneman 7

such a standard form "almost inevitably encourages dull, formulaic writing" (Irmscher 97) and that, when these forms are taught, "all of the students seemed to write exactly alike" (104). By focusing on formulaic essays, teachers encourage convergent thinking by giving students the impression that there is only one correct way to write. In a 1990 article printed by the English Journal, John Dinan says that students "believe that barren, formulaic writing is what we want from them. Standardized tests of English cultivate this belief [. . .] because they implicitly define the writing process as mechanistic and impersonal" (54). The concept of writing as a mechanical process is very different from that advocated in Rief's ideal classroom.

¶9   As dull as these exercises are for teachers to grade, they are even duller for students to write. Rief makes the comment, "I cannot immerse my students in literature I don't like, any more than any of us can write effectively on topics in which we have little interest" (19). One of the sample prompts Rison gives for fourth graders consists of a picture of a man sitting in a hole eating a sandwich. Beside him lie a pick and a lunchbox. The caption says, "This is a picture of a construction worker. Look at this picture and describe what you see on two sheets" (143). Is this topic supposed to produce a student's best writing? Are there aspects of a construction worker's life to which fourth graders can relate their own experiences? Why should they care about the construction worker at all? Nothing in this exercise has any application beyond preparation for answering similarly bland test prompts in the future. When confronted with one such prompt, Rief cut it out of the test books for her class and replaced it with "Write about anything you care deeply about. Try to convince the reader how much you care" (121).

¶10   The prompts Rison gives for tenth graders are not much better: "Your school wants to add a new course. Your principal has asked for suggestions. Write a letter to your principal telling what courses you would add and give convincing reasons for your choice" (180). The work can seem mindless. Students in Maryland were forced to sit through drill sessions even after they had passed the state-mandated tests for graduation (Corbett). Imagine, day after day of tedious prompt writing for no purpose whatsoever. No wonder Dinan complains,

> To take such a test is to become bored,
> to become a machine--that is, to take
> on the characteristics of a dull,
> lifeless writer [. . .] most students
> simply don't like writing very much,
> they are apprehensive about it,
> beleaguered by it, inclined to do it
> only on demand. (55)

Drilling students for these tests undermines the writing teacher's attempts to create an environment in which students are interested in and feel comfortable with their writing.

¶11   Under these conditions students learn to hate writing. They see it as a boring chore, a task they must complete in order to please a higher authority rather than a process intended to produce something they themselves can take pride in. As soon as they learn to write the type of dry, five-paragraph essay that puts professors to sleep their growth as writers ends. The type of idyllic writing classroom Rief describes is still possible under the pressure of a high-stakes test, but it requires creative faculty willing to bet their jobs that students can pass these tests without drills. Unfortunately, when superintendents are receiving calls from angry parents whose children aren't going to graduate, what is good can take a back seat to what is expedient. In the rush to raise the scores of those who can't meet the state objectives, creativity is crushed in those who can.

Brenneman 10

Works Cited

Arni, Sherry. "I Can Live with It." English
    Journal 79 (Nov. 1990): 76.

"Chapters 110 and 128, Subchapter C." Texas
    Education Agency Administrative Rules. 1
    Sept. 1998. Texas Education Agency. 6 March
    2000 <http://www.tea.state.tx.us/rules/
    tac/ch110_128c.html>.

Corbett, H. Dickson, and Bruce L. Wilson.
    Testing, Reform, and Rebellion. Norwood:
    Ablex, 1991.

Dinan, John. "Standardized Tests: Multiple
    Choices of the Wrong Kind." English Journal
    79 (Oct. 1990): 54-56.

Garner, Donna. "RE: A Special Note on the TAAS
    Series." Online posting. 29 Jan. 2000.
    EducationNews.org Bulletin Board. 13 Feb.
    2000 <http://www.educationnews.org/cgi/
    webbbs/article/article_list.pl>.

Irmscher, William F. Teaching Expository Writing.
    New York: Holt, 1979.

Kaufhold, Jack. "What's Wrong with Teaching for
    the Test?" The School Administrator 55 (Dec.
    1998): 14-16.

Linda/tx. "RE: Teaching to the TAAS Criticism
    Getting to Me." Online posting. 4 Feb. 2000.
    Texas Teachers Chatboard. 13 Feb. 2000
    <http://texas.teachers.net/chatboard/>.

Mary. "RE: Teaching to the TAAS Criticism Getting
    to Me." Online posting. 4 Feb. 2000. Texas
    Teachers Chatboard. 13 Feb. 2000
    <http://texas.teachers.net/chatboard/>.

Melissa. "RE: Does Your School Give a Released TAAS Test?" Online posting. 14 Jan. 2000. Texas Teachers Chatboard. 13 Feb. 2000 <http://texas.teachers.net/chatboard/>.

Neill, Shirley Boes. The Competency Movement: Problems and Solutions. Sacramento, CA: Educational News Service, 1978.

Rief, Linda. Seeking Diversity. Portsmouth: Heinemann, 1992.

Rison, A. D. A. D. Rison's Teachers' and Parents' Guide to Pass the TAAS Test: Language Arts, Reading and Writing. Austin: Sunbelt, 1990.

Shaughnessy, Anne. "Teaching to the Test: Sometimes a Good Practice." English Journal 83 (Apr. 1994): 54-56.

11 | APA Style

"The imagination imitates. It is the critical spirit that creates."
—OSCAR WILDE, playwright, poet, novelist

The American Psychological Association (APA) style of documentation is used in many social sciences and related courses, such as anthropology, education, home economics, linguistics, political science, psychology, and sociology. The basic procedures for using APA style are spelled out in this chapter. A full explanation of APA procedures is provided by the *Publication Manual of the American Psychological Association,* 5th edition (2001). The APA Web site at <http://www.apa.org/> offers students software to assist in creating APA style papers.

EXPRESS!

You need to take only two steps to use APA style properly.

1. Insert an in-text note for each source you use in your project.
2. Record all sources used in these notes in a References page.

Notice in the following example how the in-text note tells readers to look for a work by Tebeaux published in 1991 on the References page.

```
Tebeaux (1991) argues that technical writing
developed in important ways during the
English Renaissance.
```

Your readers can then turn to the References page for complete publication information about the source.

```
                    References
Tebeaux, E. (1991). Ramus, visual rhetoric,
        and the emergence of page design in
        medical writing of the English
        Renaissance. Written Communication,
        8, 411-445.
```

a In-Text Citations

The main purpose of the in-text citation is to direct your reader to the original source of the information you are citing. See 11c, APA Models, for numerous examples of in-text notes and their corresponding References entries. For formatting of in-text notes, see "In-Text Citations: APA Style," page 102.

1. A work that includes an author and page number

   Most commonly, the APA note consists of the last name of the source's author, followed immediately by the year the material was published, in parentheses. Alternately, you can place both the author's last name and the date within the parentheses.

   ```
   Tebeaux (1991) argues that technical writing
   developed in important ways during the
   English Renaissance.
   ```

   ```
   Technical writing developed in important ways
   during the English Renaissance (Tebeaux,
   1991).
   ```

   You must include a page number for direct quotations, and you may choose to do so for indirect citations as well.

   ```
   During the English Renaissance, writers began
   to employ "various page design strategies to
   enhance visual access" (Tebeaux, 1991, p.
   413).
   ```

   You may also distribute the citation information throughout.

   ```
   Tebeaux (1991) observes that for writers in
   the late sixteenth century, the philosophical
   ideas of Peter Ramus "provided a significant
   impetus to major changes in page design" (p.
   413).
   ```

2. More than one work written by an author in a single year

   Assign a lowercase letter after the date to distinguish between the two works.

   ```
   (Rosner, 1991a)
   ```

   ```
   (Rosner, 1991b)
   ```

```
The charge is raised by Rosner (1991a),
quickly answered by Anderson (1991), and then
raised again by Rosner (1991b).
```

3. More than one work in a single note

Separate the citations with a semicolon and list them in alphabetical order.

```
(Searle, 1993; Yamibe, 1995)
```

4. A whole Web site

Give the electronic address in the paper; the site does not need to be included in the References list. (This form cannot be used, however, if you are citing a particular Web document.)

```
More information about psychology as a
profession is available on the American
Psychological Association's Web site at
http://www.apa.org/.
```

5. Two or more sources in a single sentence

Insert the notes directly after the statements they support.

```
While Porter (1981) suggests that the ecology
of the aquifer might be hardier than
suspected, "given the size of the drainage
area and the nature of the subsurface rock"
(p. 62), there is no reason to believe that
the county needs another shopping mall in an
area described as "one of the last outposts
of undisturbed nature in the state"
(Martinez, 1982, p. 28).
```

6. A single source provides a series of references

There is no need to repeat the name of the author until other sources interrupt the series. After the first reference, use only page numbers until another citation intervenes. Even then, if the references all occur in a single paragraph, repeat only the author's last name (without the date).

```
The council vetoed zoning approval for a mall
in an area described by Martinez (1982) as
the last outpost of undisturbed nature in the
state. The area provides a "unique
```

environment for several endangered species of
birds and plant life" (p. 31). The birds,
especially the endangered vireo, require
breeding spaces free from encroaching
development (Harrison & Cafiero, 1979). Rare
plant life is similarly endangered
(Martinez).

7. **Quotations of forty words or more**

   Indent a long quotation five spaces from the left margin,
   omit quotation marks, and place the parenthetical note outside the final punctuation mark.

Mansfield (1998) explains this effect of
trauma on cognition:

> During normal experience, literal images
> are evaluated for meaning, placed in a
> narrative, and stripped of extraneous
> information. The symbolic image that
> results contains only the details that
> are essential for the memory to make
> sense. During a traumatic experience
> this processing is impaired. (p. 4)

In-Text Citations: APA Style

- A comma and a space separate the author's last name and the date of publication: (Martinez, 1982)
- The abbreviation *p.* or *pp.* and a space precede a page number or numbers: (Martinez, 1982, p. 31)
- If the source has two authors, their last names are joined by an ampersand: (Harrison & Cafiero, 1979)
- If you need to cite more than one work written by an author in a single year, assign a lowercase letter after the date to distinguish between the author's two works: (Rosner, 1991a), (Rosner, 1991b)
- The note itself falls *outside* the quotation marks: " . . . " (Rosner, 1991a)
- The final punctuation for the sentence comes *after* the note: (Rosner, 1991b).*

*Exception: If a quotation is 40 words or longer, see #7, above.

b The References Page

On a separate page at the end of your project, list alphabetically every source you used directly, except for personal communications. Title the list "References."

References Page: APA Style

- Center the title "References" at the top of the page, with no quotation marks.
- Arrange the items alphabetically by the last name of the author. Give initials only for first names. If no author is given, list the work according to the first word in the title (excluding *The, A,* and *An*).
- List two or more entries by the same author by year of publication, from earliest to latest. If one author publishes two works in the same year, list them alphabetically by title.
- Make first line of each entry flush with the left-hand margin. Subsequent lines in an entry are indented five spaces.
- Double-space the list. Students are permitted to single space individual entries, but the double space is preserved between entries.
- Punctuate items carefully. Remember that a period ends each entry—except those that terminate with an electronic address.
- Capitalize only the first word and any proper names in the title of a book or article. Within a title, capitalize the first word after a colon.

```
                    Genome Project      10
                  References
Baker, C. (1997). Your genes, your
      choices. American Association for the
      Advancement of Science. Retrieved
      July 16, 1997, from http://www
      .nextwave.org/ehr/books/index.html
Caskey, T. C. (1994). Human genes: The map
      takes shape. Patient Care, 28, 28-32.
Conn, L. (1996). Human genome education
      project. 1996 DOE Human Genome
      Program Contractor-Grantee Workshop
      v. Abstract retrieved July 18, 1997,
```

(continued)

```
      from http://www.ornl.gov/
      TechResources/Human_Genome/publicat/
      96santa/elsi/conn.html
Davis, J. (1990). Mapping the code: The
      Human Genome Project and the choices
      of modern science. New York: Wiley.
```

c   APA Models

Below you will find APA models to follow in creating in-text notes and the corresponding References entries for numerous kinds of sources. Simply locate the type of source you need to cite in the APA Models Index and then locate that item by number in the list that follows.

APA Models Index

65. Book, one author
66. Book, two authors
67. Book, three or more authors
68. Book, revised
69. Book, edited
70. Book with no author
71. Book, a collection or anthology
72. Work within a collection, anthology, or reader
73. Chapter in a book
74. Book review
75. Article in a scholarly journal paginated by year or volume, not issue by issue
76. Article in a monthly periodical paginated issue by issue
77. Article in a weekly or biweekly periodical
78. Article in a newsletter
79. Article in a periodical—author not named
80. Newspaper article—author named
81. Newspaper article—author not named
82. Computer software
83. Online source, archived listserv, or Usenet
84. WWW page—generic
85. WWW page—online scholarly article
86. WWW page—online newspaper article
87. WWW page—online abstract
88. Email
89. Movie/videotape/DVD
90. Musical recording

65. Book, One Author—APA

Notes:

```
Pearson (1949) found . . .

(Pearson, 1949)

(Pearson, 1949, p. 49)
```

```
                References
Pearson, G. (1949). Emotional disorders of
     children. Annapolis, MD: Naval Institute
     Press.
```

66. Book, Two Authors—APA

Notes:

```
Lasswell and Kaplan (1950) found . . .

(Lasswell & Kaplan, 1950)

(Lasswell & Kaplan, 1950, pp. 210-213)
```

```
                References
Lasswell, H. D., & Kaplan, A. (1950). Power
     and society: A framework for political
     inquiry. New York: Yale University
     Press.
```

67. Book, Three or More Authors—APA

```
First note: Rosenberg, Gerver, & Howton (1971)
found . . .
Subsequent notes: Rosenberg et al. (1971)
found . . .

First note: (Rosenberg, Gerver, & Howton, 1971)
Subsequent notes: (Rosenberg et al., 1971)
```

```
                References
Rosenberg, B., Gerver, I., & Howton, F. W.
     (1971). Mass society in crisis: Social
     problems and social pathology (2nd ed.).
     New York: Macmillan.
```

If a work has six or more authors, use the first author's name
followed by *et al.* for all parenthetical references, including
the first. In the References list, however, identify all the authors.

68. Book, Revised—APA

Notes:

Edelmann (1969) found . . .

(Edelmann, 1969)

(Edelmann, 1969, p. 62)

References

Edelmann, A. T. (1969). *Latin American*
        government and politics (Rev. ed.).
        Homewood, IL: Dorsey.

69. Book, Edited—APA

Notes:

Journet and Kling (1984) observe . . .

(Journet & Kling, 1984)

References

Journet, D., & Kling, J. (Eds.). (1984).
        Readings for technical writers.
        Glenview, IL: Scott, Foresman.

70. Book, No Author—APA

Notes:

In *Illustrated Atlas* (1985) . . .

(*Illustrated Atlas*, 1985, pp. 88-89)

References

Illustrated atlas of the world. (1985).
        Chicago: Rand McNally.

When the author of a work is actually listed as "Anonymous," cite the work that way in the References list and parenthetical note.

(Anonymous, 1995)

71. **Book, a Collection or Anthology—APA**

    Notes:

    ```
    Feinstein (1967) found . . .

    (Feinstein, 1967)
    ```

                         References
    ```
    Feinstein, C. H. (Ed.). (1967). Socialism,
            capitalism, and economic growth.
            Cambridge, England: Cambridge University
            Press.
    ```

72. **Work Within a Collection, Anthology, or Reader—APA**
    List the item on the References page by the author of the piece
    you are actually citing, not the editor(s) of the collection.

    Notes:

    ```
    Patel (1967) found . . .

    (Patel, 1967)
    ```

                         References
    ```
    Patel, S. (1967). World economy in transition
            (1850-2060). In C. H. Feinstein (Ed.),
            Socialism, capitalism, and economic
            growth (pp. 255-270). Cambridge,
            England: Cambridge University Press.
    ```

73. **Chapter in a Book—APA**

    Notes:

    ```
    Clark (1969) observes . . .

    (Clark, 1969)
    ```

                         References
    ```
    Clark, K. (1969). Heroic materialism. In
            Civilisation (pp. 321-347). New York:
            HarperCollins.
    ```

74. **Book Review—APA**

    Notes:

    ```
    Max (1999) claims . . .

    (Max, 1999)
    ```

References

Max, D. T. (1999, December 27). All the
    world's an I.P.O.: Shakespeare the
    profiteer [Review of the book
    *Shakespeare's 21st-century economics:
    The morality of love and money*]. *The New
    York Observer*, p. 35.

If a review is untitled, identify the author and date and describe the item in brackets.

Notes:

Farquhar (1987) observes . . .

(Farquhar, 1987)

References

Farquhar, J. (1987). [Review of the book
    Medical power and social knowledge].
    American Journal of Psychology, 94, 256.

75. **Article in a Scholarly Journal—APA**   Scholarly journals are usually identified by volume number or season (rather than day, week, or month of publication) and are paginated year by year, with a full year's work gathered and treated as a volume. Cite articles from such scholarly journals by providing author, date, title of article, journal, volume, and page numbers.

Notes:

Tebeaux (1991) observes . . .

(Tebeaux, 1991, p. 411)

References

Tebeaux, E. (1991). Ramus, visual rhetoric,
    and the emergence of page design in
    medical writing of the English
    Renaissance. *Written Communication, 8,*
    411–445.

76. **Article in a Monthly Periodical—APA**

Notes:

Greenstein (2000) notes . . .

(Greenstein, 2000)

References

Greenstein, J. (2000, February). Snow job.
     Brill's Content, 3, 70-77.

77. Article in a Weekly or Biweekly Periodical—APA

Notes:

Lasch-Quinn (2000) observes . . .

(Lasch-Quinn, 2000)

(Lasch-Quinn, 2000, p. 37)

References

Lasch-Quinn, E. (2000, March 6). Mothers and
     markets. *The New Republic, 222,* 37-44.

78. Article in a Newsletter—APA

Notes:

Piedmont-Marton (1997) argues . . .

(Piedmont-Marton, 1997)

References

Piedmont-Marton, E. (1997, July 20).
     Schoolmarms or language paramedics? *The
     Writer's Block, 4,* 6.

79. Article in a Periodical, No Author Named—APA

Notes:

In "Aladdin releases" (1993) . . .

("Aladdin releases," 1993)

References

Aladdin releases desktop tools. (1993,
     October). *Macworld, 10,* 35.

80. Newspaper Article, Author Named—APA   If the article
does not appear on consecutive pages in the newspaper, give
all the page numbers. Abbreviations for *page* (*p.*) and *pages*
(*pp.*) are used with newspaper entries.

Notes:

Bragg (1994) reports . . .

(Bragg, 1994, p. 7A)

References

Bragg, R. (1994, October 15). Weather gurus
going high-tech. *San Antonio Express-
News,* pp. 1A, 7A.

81. **Newspaper Article, No Author Named—APA**

Notes:

In the article "Scientists find" (1994) . . .

("Scientists find," 1994)

References

Scientists find new dinosaur species in
Africa. (1994, October 14). *The Daily
Texan,* p. 3.

82. **Computer Software—APA**   List authors only when they
own the product.

Note:

In Adobe Pagemill (1995) . . .

References

Adobe Pagemill 1.0 [Computer software].
(1995). Mountain View, CA: Adobe
Systems.

83. **Online Source, Archived Listserv, or Usenet Newsgroup—
APA**   For all online sources, provide the same information
you would give for printed sources. Then, if helpful, identify
the "medium" of the source in brackets, that is, the kind of material it is. Finally, furnish the date of access and a path statement to guide readers to the material, usually an electronic address or the protocol, directory, and file name of the source.

Notes:

Dubrowski (1994) reports . . .

(Dubrowski, 1994)

References

Dubrowski, J. (1994, October 18). Mixed
signals from Washington leave
automakers puzzled [Clarinet news item].
Retrieved October 20, 1995, from

C-reuters@clarinet.com. Directory:
biz/industry/automotive

84. **WWW Page—APA**

Notes:

Johnson (1997) explains . . .

(Johnson, 1997)

References

Johnson, C. W., Jr. (1997, February 13). *How
our laws are made*. Retrieved May 27,
1997, from http://thomas.loc.gov/home/
lawsmade.toc.html

85. **WWW Page—Online Scholarly Article—APA**

No bracketed explanation of the medium is necessary.
Notes:

Fine and Kurdek (1993) report . . .

(Fine & Kurdek, 1993)

References

Fine, M. A., & Kurdek, L. A. (1993).
Reflections on determining authorship
credit and authorship order on faculty-
student collaborations. *American
Psychologist, 48,* 1141-1147. Retrieved
July 17, 1997, from http://www.apa.org/
journals/amp/kurdek.html

86. **WWW Page—Online Newspaper Article—APA**

Notes:

Cohen (1997) asks . . .

(Cohen, 1997)

References

Cohen, E. (1997, January 17). Shrinks aplenty
online but are they credible? *The New
York Times on the Web.* Retrieved May 5,

```
1997, from http://search.nytimes.com/
search
```

87. **WWW Page—Online Abstract—APA**

Notes:
```
Shilkret and Nigrosh (1997) report . . .

(Shilkret & Nigrosh, 1997)
```

References
```
Shilkret, R., & Nigrosh, E. (1997). Assessing
    students' plans for college. Journal of
    Counseling Psychology, 44, 222-231.
    Abstract retrieved July 1, 1997, from
    http://www.apa.org/journals/cov/497ab
    .html#10
```

88. **Email—APA**   Electronic communications not stored or archived have limited use for researchers. APA style treats such information (as well as email) like personal communication. Make no mention of these sources in the References list. However, acknowledge them in the body of the essay in parenthetical notes.

```
According to Rice (personal communication,
October 14, 1994) . . .
```

89. **Movie/Videotape/DVD—APA**   This is also the basic form for audiotapes, slides, charts, and other nonprint sources. The specific medium is described between brackets, as shown here for a film. In most cases, APA references are listed by identifying the screenwriter.

Notes:
```
McCanlies (1998) features . . .

(McCanlies, 1998)
```

References
```
McCanlies, T. (Screenwriter). (1998).
    Dancer, Texas [Film]. Culver City, CA:
    TriStar.
```

90. **Musical Recording—APA**

Note:

```
In the song "What Was It You Wanted?" (Dylan,
1989, track 10) . . .
```

```
                  References
Dylan, B. (1989). What was it you wanted?
     [Recorded by Willie Nelson]. On Across
     the borderline [CD]. New York: Columbia.
```

d   Sample APA Pages

For a sample References list, see page 103. To view complete research papers in APA style, visit *Psyche-E*, an online psychology journal for undergraduates, at <http://www.siu.edu/departments/cola/psycho/journal>.

1. **Title page**

    APA style requires a separate title page; use the model below and review the following checklist.

    - Type your paper on white bond paper. Preferred typefaces (when you have a choice) include Times Roman, American Typewriter, and Courier.
    - Number the title page and all subsequent pages in the upper right-hand corner. Place a short title for the paper before the page number; the short title is the first two or three words of the title.
    - Center the title, your name (first name, middle initial, last name), and your school name as shown in the model.
    - In the title, capitalize all important words and all words of four letters or more. Do not underline or boldface the title, and do not use all capitals.

```
                          Genome Project     1


     The Genome Project: Opportunities and Ethics
                    Gerald J. Reuter
          The University of Texas at Austin
```

2. Abstract

An abstract is a concise summary of the paper. Abstracts are common in papers using APA style. When preparing an abstract, consult the model below and review the following checklist.

- Place the abstract on a separate page, after the title page.
- Center the word "Abstract" at the top of the page, without quotation marks.
- Include the short title and page number (2) in the upper right-hand corner.
- Double-space the abstract.
- Do not indent the first line; type the abstract in block form.
- Strict APA form limits abstracts to 960 characters or fewer (about 120 words).

                                    Genome Project   2
                            Abstract
Begun in 1988, the human genome project intends
to map the 23 chromosomes that provide the
blueprint for the human species. The project has
both scientific and ethical goals. The scientific
goals underscore the advantages of the genome
project, including identifying and curing
diseases and enabling people to select the traits
of their offspring, among other opportunities.
Ethically, however, the project raises serious
questions about the morality of genetic
engineering. To handle both the medical
opportunities and ethical dilemmas posed by the
genome project, scientists need to develop a
clear set of principles for genetic engineering
and to continue educating the public about the
genome project.

12 Chicago Style

"To a historian, libraries are food, shelter, and even muse." —BARBARA TUCHMAN, historian

Writers who prefer full footnotes or endnotes rather than in-text notes often use the "humanities style" of documentation recommended in *The Chicago Manual of Style* (14th ed., 1993). Basic procedures for this system are spelled out in this chapter. If you need further information or prefer the author-date style of Chicago documentation, consult the full manual or *A Manual for Writers of Term Papers, Theses, and Dissertations* (6th ed., 1996). For answers to general questions about editing, or Chicago style specifically, check out the FAQ supported by the manuscript editing department at the University of Chicago Press at <http://www.press.uchicago.edu/Misc/Chicago/cmosfaq.html>.

EXPRESS!

You need to take only three basic steps to use Chicago style properly.

1. Place a raised number after any sentence or clause you need to document.
2. Link every note number to a note.
3. Record all sources in a bibliographic list. (This step is sometimes optional; consult your instructor.)

The raised (superscript number) after the quotation in the following example leads the reader to a corresponding note 1.

```
Athena gives Diomedes "courage and boldness,
to make him come to the front and cover
himself in glory."1
```

To find complete publication information, your readers can then turn to note 1.

```
    1. Homer, The Iliad, trans. Robert
Fitzgerald (New York: Anchor Press, 1974),
58.
```

Chicago Style allows you to use either footnotes (at the bottom of the page) or endnotes (at the end of the paper), although you must be consistent throughout your paper—these two types of notes can't be mixed.

If a bibliographic list—Works Cited or Bibliography—is also required, your reader will find similar information in a slightly different format there.

> Homer, *The Iliad.* Translated by Robert
>   Fitzgerald. New York: Anchor Press, 1974.

Chicago allows for two styles of bibliography pages: Works Cited or Bibliography. If you will list only the sources directly cited in your project, use the term "Works Cited" to head your references list. If you will list all the sources you consulted in your research, use the term "Bibliography."

a In-Text Citations and Notes

The purpose of the in-text citation is to direct your reader to the note, which includes the original source of the information you are citing. In the text, place a raised (superscript) number after the material you need to document. The numbers run consecutively throughout the paper. (To create such a raised number, select "superscript" from your word-processing font options.) See 12c, Chicago Models, for examples of notes. For formatting of in-text citations and notes, see "In-Text Citations and Notes: Chicago Style," page 117.

1. Two or more sources in a single sentence

The note numbers appear right after the statements they support.

> While some in the humanities fear that
> electronic technologies may make the "notion
> of wisdom" obsolete,[2] others suggest that
> technology must be the subject of serious
> study even in elementary and secondary
> school.[3]

The notes for this sentence would appear as follows.

>   2. Sven Birkerts, *The Gutenberg Elegies:
> The Fate of Reading in an Electronic Age*
> (Boston: Faber and Faber, 1994), 139.

        3. Neil Postman, "The Word Weavers/The
World Makers," in *The End of Education:
Redefining the Value of School* (New York:
Alfred A. Knopf, 1995), 172-93.

Observe that note 2 documents a particular quotation while note 3 refers to a full book chapter.

2. One work several times in a project

The first note gives full information about author(s), title, and publication.

        1. Helen Wilkinson, "It's Just a Matter
of Time," *Utne Reader* (May/June 1995): 66-67.

Then, in shorter papers, any subsequent citations require only the last name of the author(s) and page number(s).

        3. Wilkinson, 66.

In longer papers, the entry may also include a shortened title to make references from page to page easier to follow.

        3. Wilkinson, "Matter of Time," 66.

If you cite the same work again immediately after a full note, you may use the Latin abbreviation *Ibid.* (meaning "in the same place"), followed by the page number(s) of the citation.

        1. James Morgan, "Blue Highways," in *The
Distance to the Moon* (New York: Riverhead,
1999), 93.

        2. Ibid., 89.

To avoid using *Ibid.* when documenting the same source in succession, simply use a page reference—for example, (89)—within the text itself. When successive citations are to exactly the same page, *Ibid.* alone can be used.

In-Text Citations and Notes: Chicago Style

- Raised numbers in the text follow any punctuation marks, except for dashes: ". . . with glory."[6]
- Place notes either at the bottom of each page (footnotes), or in a single list titled "Notes" at the end of your paper (endnotes).
- Single-space individual notes, and double-space between notes.
- Indent the first line of each note like a paragraph.

(continued)

In-Text Citations and Notes: Chicago Style (continued)

• Use either underlines or italics for titles of longer works, but don't mix the two styles in your project.

                    Notes

    1. Helen Wilkinson, "It's Just a Matter of Time," *Utne Reader* (May/June 1995): 66-67.

    2. Paul Osterman, "Getting Started," *Wilson Quarterly* (autumn 1994): 46-55.

    3. James Morgan, "Blue Highways," in *The Distance to the Moon* (New York: Riverhead, 1999), 93.

    4. Ibid., 97.

    5. Wilkinson, 66.

    6. Ibid.

    7. Ibid., 67.

Notice that note 4 refers to the Morgan chapter and notes 6 and 7 refer to Wilkinson's article.

b Chicago Bibliographies

At the end of your project, list alphabetically every source cited or used in the paper. Title the list "Works Cited" if it includes only works actually mentioned in the essay; title it "Bibliography" if it also includes works consulted in preparing the project but not actually cited. Because Chicago notes are quite thorough, a Works Cited or Bibliography page may be optional; consult your instructor.

When an author has more than one work on the list, arrange them alphabetically under the author's name using this form.

    Altick, Richard D. *The Shows of London.* Cambridge: Belknap-Harvard University Press, 1978.

    ---. *Victorian People and Ideas.* New York: Norton, 1973.

    ---. *Victorian Studies in Scarlet.* New York: Norton, 1977.

Bibliographies: Chicago Style

- Center the title ("Works Cited" or "Bibliography") at the top of a new page after the end of your piece. Don't use quotation marks around the title.
- Single-space within each entry; double-space between entries.
- Arrange the list alphabetically by author's last name.
- Start each entry at the left margin; indent subsequent lines of an entry like a paragraph.

Works Cited

```
Frazer, R. M. A Reading of "The Iliad."
     Lanham, Md.: University Press of
     America, 1993.

Homer. The Iliad. Translated by Robert
     Fitzgerald. New York: Anchor Press,
     1974.

Kirk, G. S. "The Iliad": A Commentary. Vol.
     2. New York: Cambridge Univ. Press,
     1990.

Toohey, Peter. "Epic and Rhetoric: Speech-
     making and Persuasion in Homer and
     Apollonius." Arachnion: A Journal of
     Ancient Literature and History on the
     Web 1 (1995). Journal online.
     Available from http://www.cisi.unito
     .it/arachne/num1/toohey.html;
     Internet; accessed 21 February 1996.
```

c Chicago Models

In this section, you will find the Chicago notes and bibliography forms for more than twenty types of sources. The numbered items in the list are the sample note forms, often showing the specific page numbers as you would when preparing actual notes; the matching bibliography entries appear immediately after.

Chicago Models Index

(continued)

Chicago Models Index (continued)

91. Book, One Author—Chicago

1. Steven Weinberg, *Dreams of a Final Theory* (New York: Pantheon Books, 1992), 38.

Weinberg, Steven. *Dreams of a Final Theory*. New York: Pantheon Books, 1992.

92. Book, Two or Three Authors or Editors—Chicago

2. Peter Collier and David Horowitz, *Destructive Generation: Second Thoughts about the '60s* (New York: Summit, 1989), 24.

Collier, Peter, and David Horowitz. *Destructive Generation: Second Thoughts about the '60s.* New York: Summit, 1989.

93. Book, Four or More Authors or Editors—Chicago Use *et al.* or *and others* after the first author in the notes, but list all authors in the bibliography when that is convenient.

3. Philip Curtin and others, eds., *African History* (Boston: Little, Brown, 1978), 77.

Curtin, Philip, Steve Feierman, Leonard Thompson, and Jan Vansina, eds. *African History*. Boston: Little, Brown, 1978.

94. Book, Edited—Focus on the Editor—Chicago

4. Scott Elledge, ed., *Paradise Lost*, by John Milton (New York: Norton, 1975).

Elledge, Scott, ed. *Paradise Lost,* by John Milton. New York: Norton, 1975.

95. Book, Edited—Focus on the Original Author—Chicago

> 5. William Shakespeare, *The Complete Works of Shakespeare,* 4th ed., ed. David Bevington (New York: Longman, 1997).

Shakespeare, William. *The Complete Works of Shakespeare.* 4th ed. Edited by David Bevington. New York: Longman, 1997.

96. Book Written by a Group—Chicago

> 6. Council of Biology Editors, *Scientific Style and Format: The CBE Manual for Authors, Editors, and Publishers,* 6th ed. (Cambridge: Cambridge Univ. Press, 1994).

Council of Biology Editors. *Scientific Style and Format: The CBE Manual for Authors, Editors, and Publishers.* 6th ed. Cambridge: Cambridge Univ. Press, 1994.

97. Book with No Author—Chicago List it by its title, excluding *The, A,* or *An.*

> 7. *Webster's Collegiate Thesaurus.* (Springfield: Merriam, 1976).

Webster's Collegiate Thesaurus. Springfield: Merriam, 1976.

98. Work of More Than One Volume—Chicago

> 8. Karlheinz Spindler, *Abstract Algebra with Applications* (New York: Dekker, 1994), 1:17–18.

Spindler, Karlheinz. *Abstract Algebra with Applications.* Vol. 1. New York: Dekker, 1994.

99. Work in a Series—Chicago

> 9. Grayson Kirk and Nils H. Wessell, eds., *The Soviet Threat: Myths and Realities,* Proceedings of the Academy of Political Science, no. 33 (New York: Academy of Political Science, 1978), 62.

Kirk, Grayson, and Nils H. Wessell, eds. *The Soviet Threat: Myths and Realities.* Proceedings of the Academy of Political Science, no. 33. New York: Academy of Political Science, 1978.

100. Chapter in a Book—Chicago

10. Delia Owens and Mark Owens, "Home to the Dunes," in *The Eye of the Elephant: An Epic Adventure in the African Wilderness* (Boston: Houghton Mifflin, 1992), 11–27.

Owens, Delia, and Mark Owens. "Home to the Dunes," *In The Eye of the Elephant: An Epic Adventure in the African Wilderness.* Boston: Houghton Mifflin, 1992.

101. Article in a Scholarly Journal—Chicago

Scholarly journals are usually identified by volume number or season (rather than day, week, or month of publication). Such journals are usually paginated year by year, with a year's work treated as a volume. Provide author(s), title of the work (in quotation marks), name of periodical (underlined or italicized), volume number, date of publication, and page numbers.

11. Karl P. Wentersdorf, "Hamlet's Encounter with the Pirates," *Shakespeare Quarterly* 34 (1983): 434–48.

Wentersdorf, Karl P. "Hamlet's Encounter with the Pirates." *Shakespeare Quarterly* 34 (1983): 434–48.

102. Article in a Popular Magazine—Chicago

12. Don Graham, "Wayne's World," *Texas Monthly,* March 2000, 110–11.

Graham, Don. "Wayne's World." *Texas Monthly,* March 2000, 110–11.

When an article does not appear on consecutive pages omit page numbers in the bibliography entry.

103. Article or Selection from a Reader or Anthology—Chicago

13. Pamela Samuelson, "The Digital Rights War," in *The Presence of Others,* 3d ed., ed. Andrea Lunsford and John Ruszkiewicz (New York: St. Martin's, 2000), 315–20.

Samuelson, Pamela. "The Digital Rights War." In *The Presence of Others.* 3d ed., edited by Andrea Lunsford and John Ruszkiewicz. New York: St. Martin's, 2000.

104. Article in a Newspaper—Chicago   Identify the edition of the paper cited (*final edition, home edition, Western edition*), except when citing editorials or features that appear in all editions. Since an individual story may move in location from edition to edition, page numbers are not ordinarily provided. Section numbers are given for papers so divided. Individual news stories are usually not listed in a bibliography.

> 14. Celestine Bohlen, "A Stunned Venice Surveys the Ruins of a Beloved Hall," *New York Times,* 31 January 1995, national edition, sec. B.

105. Encyclopedia—Chicago   When a reference work is familiar (encyclopedias, dictionaries, thesauruses), omit the names of authors and editors and most publishing information. No page number is given when a work is arranged alphabetically; instead the item referenced is named, following the abbreviation *s.v.* (*sub verbo,* meaning "under the word"). Familiar reference works are not listed in the bibliography.

> 15. *The Oxford Companion to English Literature,* 4th ed., s.v. "Locke, John."

106. Biblical Citation—Chicago   Biblical citations appear in notes but not in the bibliography. If important, you may mention the version of the Bible cited.

> 16. John 18.37-38 Jerusalem Bible.

107. Computer Software—Chicago

> 17. FoxPro Ver. 2.5, Microsoft, Seattle, Wash.

> FoxPro Ver. 2.5. Microsoft, Seattle, Wash.

108. Electronic Sources—Chicago   The standards for electronic documentation are in flux. In *The Chicago Manual of Style* (14th ed.), the examples of notes for electronic sources generally include three features: a description of the computer source in brackets, such as [*electronic bulletin board*] or [*Web site*]; the date the material was accessed, updated, or cited [*cited 28 May 1996*]; and an electronic address, following the words *available from.* Models 108–111 on page 124 follow these recommendations as modified in Kate L. Turabian's *Manual of Style for Writers of Term Papers, Theses, and Dissertations* (6th ed., 1996).

18. Sylvia Atore Alva, "Differential Patterns of Achievement Among Asian-American Adolescents," *Journal of Youth and Adolescence* 22 (1993): 407-23, *ProQuest General Periodicals* [CD-ROM], UMI-ProQuest, June 1994.

Alva, Sylvia Atore. "Differential Patterns of Achievement Among Asian-American Adolescents." *Journal of Youth and Adolescence* 22 (1993): 407-23, *ProQuest General Periodicals* [CD-ROM], UMI-ProQuest, June 1994.

109. WWW—Book Online—Chicago

19. Amelia E. Barr, *Remember the Alamo* [book online] (New York: Dodd, Mead, 1888); available from http://etext.lib.virginia .edu/; Internet; cited 12 May 1997.

Barr, Amelia E. *Remember the Alamo.* Book online. New York: Dodd, Mead, 1888. Available from http://etext.lib.virginia .edu/; Internet; cited 12 May 1997.

110. WWW—Article Online—Chicago

20. Paul Skowronek, "Left and Right for Rights," *Trincoll Journal,* 13 March 1997 [journal online]; available from http://www .trincoll.edu/~tj/tj03.13.97/articles/comm2 .html; Internet; accessed 23 July 1997.

Skowronek, Paul. "Left and Right for Rights." *Trincoll Journal,* 13 March 1997. Journal online. Available from http:// www.trincoll.edu/~tj/tj03.13.97/articles/ comm2.html; Internet; accessed 23 July 1997.

111. Email—Chicago

21. Robert D. Royer, "Re: Are We in a State of NOMAIL?" Email to author, 22 July 1997.

Royer, Robert D. "Re: Are We in a State of NOMAIL?" Email to author, 22 July 1997.

d Sample Chicago Pages

For a sample Works Cited list, see page 119. For a sample list of notes, see page 118.

1. Title page

In numbering Chicago papers, count the title page as a page, but do not number it.

Sample Title Page

```
        THE UNIVERSITY OF TEXAS AT AUSTIN
          DIOMEDES AS HERO OF THE ILIAD
            E 309--TOPICS IN WRITING
        DIVISION OF RHETORIC AND COMPOSITION
                        BY
              JEREMY A. CORLEY
              28 FEBRUARY 1996
```

On the page following the title page, repeat the title, but use capital and lowercase letters.

2. Footnotes

Here are the last several lines of a page, followed by footnotes.

Footnotes

relatively unimportant as an insult, even a public one.[4] A soldier's duty is to defend his homeland and fight in its wars, and Achilles misses

---

1. Homer, *The Iliad,* trans. Robert Fitzgerald (New York: Anchor Press, 1974), 14.

2. R. M. Frazer, *A Reading of "The Iliad"* (Lanham, Md.: University Press of America, 1993), 12.

3. Homer, 15.

4. Frazer, 11.

13 CBE Style

"To spell out the obvious is often to call it into question."

—ERIC HOFFER, writer, philosopher, longshoreman

Disciplines that study the physical world—physics, chemistry, biology—are called the *natural sciences*; disciplines that examine (and produce) technologies are described as the *applied sciences*. Writing in these fields is specialized, and no survey of all forms of documentation can be provided here. For more information about writing in the following fields, we suggest that you consult one of these style manuals.

- **Chemistry:** *The ACS Style Guide: A Manual for Authors and Editors,* 2nd edition (1998)—American Chemical Society
- **Geology:** *Suggestions to Authors of Reports of the United States Geological Survey,* 7th edition (1991)—U.S. Geological Survey
- **Mathematics:** *A Manual for Authors of Mathematical Papers,* revised edition (1990)—American Mathematical Society
- **Physics:** *AIP Style Manual,* 4th edition (1990)—American Institute of Physics

A highly influential manual for scientific writing is *Scientific Style and Format: The CBE Manual for Authors, Editors, and Publishers* (6th edition, 1994). In this chapter we briefly describe one of the two major methods of documentation advocated in the *CBE Manual*: the citation-sequence system.

EXPRESS!

There are two basic steps in the citation-sequence system.

1. In the text, use a raised number (the preferred form) or a number in parentheses to indicate a citation.

   ```
   Oncologists[1] are aware of trends in cancer
   mortality[2].
   ```

   ```
   Oncologists (1) are aware of trends in
   cancer mortality (2).
   ```

2. On a References page, give the publication information for each numbered citation in numerical order.

1. Devesa SS, Silverman DT. Cancer incidence and mortality trends in the United States: 1935-74. J Natl Cancer Inst 1978; 60:545-71.

2. Goodfield J. The siege of cancer. New York: Dell; 1978. 240 p.

a In-Text Citations

The in-text citation leads your reader to the References page, where complete publication information is listed.

1. More than one source in a single note

Separate the numbers by a hyphen if they are in sequence and by commas if they are out of sequence.

Cancer treatment[2-3] has changed over the decades. But Rettig[4] shows that the politics of cancer research remains constant.

2. Two or more citations to one source

If you cite a source again later in the paper, refer to it by its original number.

Great strides have occurred in epidemiological methods[5] despite the political problems in maintaining research support and funding described by Rettig[4].

b The References Page

On a separate page at the end of the text of your paper, list the sources you used in the order they occurred. The list is *not* alphabetical: Source 1 in the paper is the first source listed on the References page; source 2 the second item, and so on. Here is a sample References page.

References

1. Devesa SS, Silverman DT. Cancer incidence and
   mortality trends in the United States:
   1935-74. J Natl Cancer Inst 1978;60:545-71.

2. Goodfield J. The siege of cancer. New York:
   Dell; 1978. 240 p.

3. Loeb LA, Ernster VL, Warner KE, Abbotts J,
   Laszo J. Smoking and lung cancer: an overview.
   Cancer Res 1984;44:5940-58.

4. Rettig RA. Cancer crusade: the story of the
   National Cancer Act of 1971. Princeton:
   Princeton Univ Pr; 1977. 382 p.

5. Craddock VM. Nitrosamines and human cancer:
   proof of an association? Nature 1983 Dec
   15:638.

c CBE Citation-Sequence Models

Here are typical References entries for major types of sources. There are so many variations on these basic entries, however, that you will certainly want to check the *CBE Manual* when you do a major CBE-style paper.

1. **Book: CBE Citation-Sequence Entry**

   A book entry includes the following basic information.

   - Number assigned to the source.
   - Name of author(s), last name first, followed by a period. Initials are used in place of full first or middle names. Commas ordinarily separate the names of multiple authors.
   - Title of work, followed by a period. Only the first word and any proper nouns in a title are capitalized. The title is not underlined.
   - Place of publication, followed by a colon.
   - Publisher, followed by a semicolon. Titles of presses can be abbreviated.
   - Date, followed by a period.
   - Number of pages, followed by a period.

Example:

```
2. Goodfield J. The siege of cancer. New
   York: Dell; 1978. 240 p.
```

2. Scholarly Article: CBE Citation-Sequence Entry

This form is used for scholarly journals in which the pagination is continuous throughout the year. Include the following basic information.

- Number assigned to the source.
- Name of author(s), last name first, followed by a period. Initials are used in place of full first or middle names. Commas ordinarily separate the names of multiple authors.
- Title of article, followed by a period. Only the first word and any proper nouns in a title are capitalized. The title does not appear between quotation marks.
- Name of the journal. All major words are capitalized, but the journal title is not underlined. A space (but no punctuation) separates the journal title from the date. Journal titles of more than one word can be abbreviated following the recommendations in *American National Standard Z39.5–1985: Abbreviations of Titles of Publications.*
- Year (and month for journals not continuously paginated; date for weekly journals), followed immediately by a semicolon.
- Volume number, followed by a colon, and the page numbers of the article. No spaces separate these items. A period follows the page numbers.

Example:

```
1. Devesa SS, Silverman DT. Cancer incidence
   and mortality trends in the United States:
   1935-74. J Natl Cancer Inst 1978;60:545-71.
```

3. Article in a Popular Magazine: CBE Citation-Sequence Entry

Include the following basic information.

- Number assigned to the source.
- Name of author(s), last name first, followed by a period. Initials are substituted for first names unless two authors mentioned in the paper have identical last names and first initials.
- Title of article, followed by a period. Only the first word and any proper nouns in a title are capitalized. The title

does not appear between quotation marks. (Where quotation marks are needed, CBE recommends British style. See *CBE Manual,* pp. 180–81.)

- Name of magazine, abbreviated. All major words are capitalized, but the journal titles is not underlined. A space (but no punctuation) separates the magazine title from the year and month.
- Year, month (abbreviated), and day (for a weekly magazine). The year is separated from the month by a space. A colon follows immediately after the date, followed by page numbers(s). The entry ends with a period.

Example:

```
7. Zinder ND. The genome initiative: how to
   spell 'human'. Sci Am 1990 July:128.
```

4. Electronic Item

Include the basic information provided for a print document (author, title, publication information, page numbers) with the following additions.

- Electronic medium, identified between brackets. For books and monographs, this information comes after the title [*monograph online*]; for periodicals, it follows the name of the journal [*serial online*].
- Availability statement, following the publication information or page numbers.
- Date of access, if helpful in identifying what version of an electronic text was consulted.

Example:

```
9. Dewitt R. Vagueness, semantics, and the
   language of thought. PSYCHE [serial
   online] 1993 July;1(1). Available from:
   ftp.lib.ncsu.edu via the INTERNET.
   Accessed 1995 Apr 26.
```

Final Paper: CBE Style

- CBE style normally requires a separate title page. The title of the essay can be centered about a third of the way from the top of the page, followed by the word *by* on a separate line and the writer's name, also on a separate line. Other information such as instructor's name, course title, and date can be included on the bottom third of the page.

- CBE style normally requires an abstract of about 250 words on a separate sheet immediately following the title page. The title "Abstract" is centered on the page.
- Double-space the body of a CBE paper. Avoid hyphenating words at the end of the line.
- Numbering pages consecutively in the upper right-hand corner, counting the title page as the first page.
- Take special care with figures and tables. They should be numbered in separate sequences. The *CBE Manual* includes an entire chapter on handling illustrative material.
- The References page follows the text of the CBE essay on a new page. Remember that the items on this page are *not* listed alphabetically. References pages can also be titled "Literature Cited" or "References Cited."
- All works listed on the References page should be cited at least once in the body of your paper.
- Entries on the References page are single-spaced, with a space left between the entries.

PART FOUR

Sentence Revision

14 Clarity

"I'll play with it first and tell you what it is later."
— MILES DAVIS, jazz musician

Clear sentences make it easy for a careful reader to move along steadily without backtracking to puzzle about meaning. As Miles Davis suggests, though, the act of creating—whether in music or writing—may change your original intention, so you may go through several drafts before you can decide whether your ideas are stated clearly.

EXPRESS!

Bring your writing down to earth. Check your sentences to be sure you don't go too long without mentioning someone or something specific—people readers can visualize, objects they can imagine, situations they can grasp. Using specific, sensory details will help make your writing clearer.

---

a Make Your Subject Clear

Make it easy for your reader to see your subject. Ask yourself, "What is the key word or concept in the sentence?" Then see if you can make that key word the subject.

Make people or concrete things the subject.

NO PEOPLE IN SUBJECT

The excitement of doing original research has not been experienced by most first-year college students.

PEOPLE AS SUBJECT

Most first-year college students don't know the excitement of doing original research.

Replace abstract words and phrases.

ABSTRACT AND OVERLOADED SUBJECT

The inability of standardized tests, from IQ tests to SAT scores, to predict people's behavior poses a long-standing dilemma for social scientists.

PEOPLE AS SUBJECT

Social scientists have long wondered why standardized tests, from IQ tests to SAT scores, predict behavior so poorly.

b Use Vigorous Verbs

Read your draft sentence and focus on the action. Ask, "What's happening?" Whenever you can, express that action in a single lively verb.

Replace *to be* verbs with more vigorous verbs.   Forms of *be—am, is, are, was, were, being, been—*are not as interesting as verbs that do things.

OVERUSED *TO BE* VERBS

It **is** the tendency of adolescents **to be more concerned** about the opinion of others in their age group than they **are** about the values parents **are** trying to instill in them.

REPLACED WITH ACTION VERBS

Adolescents **crave** the approval of their peers and often **resist** their parents' values.

Adolescents **care** more about their friends' opinions than their parents' values.

Reduce the number of passive verbs.   Subjects perform actions in active sentences; in passive sentences, subjects receive the action. Make the subject the actor of the sentence, not the receiver.

PASSIVE VERB

Frequently, local customs ~~were ignored by the unsophisticated travelers.~~ *the unsophisticated travelers ignored*

When the action itself is more important than who performed it, or when you don't know who performed an action, retain the passive. For example, scientific and technical writing that focuses on processes and research results often requires the passive.

> Apical dominance in this rose species **was minimized** by daily pruning.

Replace cluttered verb phrases with single lively verbs.   For example, change *give consideration to* to *consider, make acknowledgment of* to *acknowledge, puts the emphasis on* to *emphasizes.*

> Some groups who ~~are in opposition to~~ ^{oppose} the death penalty ~~believe that there is doubt about~~ ^{doubt} its morality.

> Malls ~~always manage to~~ irritate me when they ~~start to~~ display Christmas paraphernalia immediately after Halloween.

c Balance Parallel Ideas

Put parallel ideas in parallel form. Sentences are easier to read when closely related ideas within them also follow similar patterns of language. Sentence elements that come in pairs or triplets should follow the same form: a noun with another noun, an adjective phrase with another adjective phrase, and so on.

Check structures that come in pairs or triplets.   Have you used the same forms for each item? If not, stack up the mismatched elements and revise any that don't fit the pattern.

NOT PARALLEL

The best doctors are **patient,**
          thorough, and
          have a lot of compassion.

PARALLEL WORDS

The best doctors are **patient, thorough,** and **compassionate.**

NOT PARALLEL

Praised by critics and
being embraced by common readers,
the novel became a best-seller.

PARALLEL PHRASES

Praised by critics, embraced by common readers, the novel became a best-seller.

NOT PARALLEL

Interest rates might be tightened, or
we might increase prices.

PARALLEL CLAUSES

Interest rates might be tightened, or **prices might be increased**.

Check items in a list for parallel structure.

PARALLEL

The school board's objectives are clear: **to hire** the best teachers, **to create** successful classrooms, **to serve** the needs of all families, and **to prepare** the students for the twenty-first century.

Use parallelism in comparisons using *as* or *than*.   Parallelism is required in comparisons following *as* or *than*.

Smiling takes fewer muscles than ~~to frown.~~ *frowning*

The city council is as likely to adopt the measure as to ~~vetoing~~ *veto* it.

Use parallelism with expressions such as *either . . . or* and *both . . . and*.   Correlatives require parallel structure. Other correlatives include *neither . . . nor, on the one hand . . . on the other hand, not only . . . but also.*

As Franklin once remarked, either **we hang together** or **we hang separately**.

d Use Specific Details

Readers will understand your ideas more easily when you use specific, concrete details: *Harley* instead of *two-wheeled vehicle* or even *motorcycle*. Obviously, you sometimes have to use abstract words to explain ideas, but for a general audience, the more specific your details, the better your piece will read. When writing for specialists, you can be more abstract.

- Replace abstract nouns with concrete nouns where possible: *building* with *farmhouse* or *brownstone*, for example.
- Replace long nouns with their shorter verb counterparts. This revision usually requires rewriting the whole sentence.

SPECIFIC DETAILS

If we don't yet breed children for their SAT scores, there is a whole class of people . . . who coach their toddlers to get into the nursery schools that offer a fast track to Harvard.
—Barbara Ehrenreich, "The Economics of Cloning"

If the writer had used an abstract phrase such as "the selection of offspring for desirable traits" to replace her more concrete example, her prose would be more difficult, not to mention more boring, to read.

State a general idea and then provide more and more specific details about it.

Toi Soldier was a magnificent black Arabian stallion, a sculpture in ebony, his eyes large and dark, his graceful head held high on an arched neck.

Use examples to illustrate general statements.

To be in love is merely to be in a state of perpetual anesthesia—to mistake an ordinary young man for a Greek god or an ordinary young woman for a goddess.
—H. L. Mencken, *Prejudices, First Series*

e State Ideas Positively

DIFFICULT TO READ
Do we have the right **not to be victims** of crime?

CLEARER
Do we have the right **to be safe** from crime?

f Chunk Your Writing

If you think readers will find a lengthy sentence hard to read, consider breaking it into shorter, more manageable ones. To present unusually complex information, consider creating a list.

In support of this proposal, they cite the example of
~~Citing an instance in which~~ a 16-year-old student ~~was~~ working 48 hours a week at Burger King in order to pay for a new car ~~and~~ *while* simultaneously trying to attend high school full time. New York educators have recently proposed legislation that prohibits high school students from working more than 3 hours on a school night, *The proposed law would* limits the total time they *students* can work in a week to 20 hours when school is in session, *would* and fines employers who violate these regulations as much as $2,000.

If your information is numerical, a graph or chart may be most effective.

Internet Users

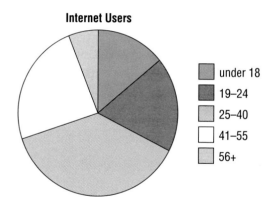

- under 18
- 19–24
- 25–40
- 41–55
- 56+

E-Tips

"Chunk size" is crucial to the success of your Web page. Readers get more impatient with material online than they do with printed matter. Use more graphic organizers—bulleted and numbered lists, quick-loading charts and figures—than you might on the printed page. Keep your sentences short and lively, and your readers may linger at your site.

DESTINATION

For more strategies for improving sentence clarity, visit the Purdue University Online Writing Lab at <http://owl.english.purdue.edu/handouts/general/gl_sentclar.html>. ■

15 Economy

"As to the Adjective: when in doubt, strike it out."   —MARK TWAIN, novelist and journalist

For those who aspire to be good writers, the war against what writer and editor William Zinsser calls "clutter" never ends. Such clutter consists of clichés, strung-out phrases, pointless repetitions, and overly detailed descriptions.

EXPRESS!

Wait until you have a first or even second draft before you start trimming your prose. Many writers overstuff a first draft because they want to get all their ideas down. That's fine: It *is* much easier to cut material than to create more.

---

a Cut Extra Words

First drafts are often filled with clichés, strung-out phrases, pointless repetitions, and dull abstractions. Prune them.

Replace sprawling phrases with single words.   Check to see if prepositional phrases and verb phrases can be condensed.

~~In the modern society in which we live today,~~ ^M^ many people still attend church regularly.

This book ~~puts an emphasis on~~ *emphasizes* the social problems caused by drug use.

Replace . . .	With . . .
in the event that	if
in light of the fact that	since
on the grounds that	because
regardless of the fact that	although
at this point in time	now
it is obvious that	obviously

on an everyday basis	routinely
is reflective of	reflects
has an understanding of	understands
is in opposition to	opposes

Cut needless redundancy.   Look for vague nouns as well as paired expressions whose elements mean the same thing.

> Our entire society has been corrupted by ~~the evil of~~ commercialism.

> *Seinfeld* ~~to me~~ is a situation comedy ~~-type show~~.

Replace . . .	With . . .
her area of specialization	her specialty
round in shape	round
belonging and togetherness	belonging
easy and effortless	easy
ready and able	ready
proper and fitting	fitting
trim and slim	trim
willing and eager	willing

Cut surplus intensifiers.   Use intensifiers only when they add weight or power to your prose.

> The Grand Canyon is a ~~quite unique~~ geological treasure, ~~basically~~ formed by the relentless power of the Colorado River.

Replace . . .	With . . .
completely finished	finished
basically done	done
totally exhausted	exhausted
awful tragedy	tragedy
absolutely pointless	pointless

Cut nominalizations.   Nominalizations are nouns made by adding endings to verbs and adjectives: *connectivity* from *connect*, *initialization* from *initial*. Restore the more lively verb or adjective by rewriting the sentence.

> *Since* ~~Given~~ the poor ~~salability of~~ some products, manufacturers often ~~have to make offerings of~~ *offer* rebates. *don't sell well*

b Cut *It is* and *There are* Sentence Openings

Using these expletives habitually will make your prose dull and amateurish.

~~There were~~ five of us huddled in the basement.

Even though ~~it is~~ the oldest of auto manufacturers, Mercedes remains innovative.

c Condense

Say more with less: Condense sentences into clauses, clauses into phrases or words.

Check for repeated elements that can be combined.

The Concours D'Elegance is an annual exhibit of classic cars, ~~The cars exhibited~~ often include handsome old Hudsons, Nashes, and Corvettes.

The geneticists had become dissatisfied with the administrator's dishonest reports of their work, ~~They~~ the geneticists published their own findings in the journal *Cell*.

Check for phrases that don't add meaning.

Thanksgiving is a time for all of us to be together ~~for the simple purpose of~~ enjoying each other's company.

Check for *who, which,* and *that.*

Ms. Rudneva, ~~who was~~ a former editor, left the company when she had twins.

DESTINATION

For ten strategies to eliminate wordiness, visit the Purdue OWL at <http://owl.english.purdue.edu/handouts/general/gl_concise.html>. ∎

16 | Variety

"Words ought to be a little wild for they are the assaults of thought on the unthinking."
—JOHN MAYNARD KEYNES, economist

Sentences should convey readers easily from point to point with clarity and emphasis. Using a variety of sentence structures allows you to guide readers to understand what is most important and relevant.

EXPRESS!

Experiment with each sentence in your draft to find a word order that creates the effect you are seeking. For example, the balance and parallelism of this sentence create a rhythm that makes the idea memorable.

Injustice anywhere is a threat to justice everywhere.
—Martin Luther King, Jr.

In this sentence, notice how the accumulating phrases allow the reader to savor each detail.

The crater spread toward the horizon, shallow and barren, ringed by flows of volcanic ash, crumbly as a dry cake.

Read your revised draft aloud to check the clarity and rhythm of the piece overall.

---

a Combine Short Sentences

If your prose seems choppy, see if you can combine related sentences with coordinate or subordinate clauses. Combining short sentences will smooth out your prose and, often, make your ideas clearer.

Check for strings of simple sentences. When many sentences in a row consist of simple subject plus verb combinations, the effect is monotony. Combine sentences with a comma and the coordinating conjunction—*and, or, nor, for, but, yet,* and *so*—that best expresses the relationship between the sentences.

SAT scores in math rose nationally, but Verbal scores dropped.
Notice the placement of the comma *before* **but**.

You can also coordinate elements within sentences.

Elizabeth Cruse is working on her résumé, ~~She is also~~ planning
her interview with New Horizons Enterprises, ~~She is~~ complet-
ing her master's degree in marketing.

Note that a comma *precedes* **and**.

The occasional short sentence, however, adds punch.

Jesus wept.

Subordinate some sentences.   Link subordinate clauses
to related independent clauses with words such as *because, until,
since, although, before, when, where, if.*

Many people go into debt, *when* Credit is easy to get.

The film enjoyed a brisk summer box office, *because* It won an Academy Award last March.

Because the film won an Academy Award last March, it enjoyed a brisk summer box office.

When a subordinate clause *precedes* the independent clause,
use a comma to set it off.

Highlight the contrast between independent clauses.
Use a semicolon and the conjunctive adverb—*however, moreover,
therefore,* and so on—that best expresses the relationship.

Members of the zoning board appreciated the developer's
arguments, *; however,* They rejected her rezoning request.

When **however** comes between two independent clauses, a
semicolon precedes it and a comma follows.

---

b Expand Simple Sentences with
Interesting Details

Not all simple sentences are short; you can expand them by
compounding or modifying their subjects (S), verbs (V), or objects (O).

	S	V	O

ORIGINAL SENTENCE   Bugs scare people.

EXPANDED S   Tiny spiders, harmless caterpillars, and frail mantises

EXPANDED V   terrify or even paralyze

EXPANDED O   full-grown adults, from Ph.D.'s in physics to NFL linebackers

REVISED SENTENCE

Tiny spiders, harmless caterpillars, and frail mantises sometimes terrify or even paralyze full-grown adults, from Ph.D.'s in physics to NFL linebackers.

Your purpose for writing will likely determine whether adding details such as these makes the sentence more effective.

c Vary Sentence Openings

Move a word, phrase, or clause to the beginning of a sentence to increase sentence variety.

Fortunately, our finances improved.

In the eyes of our children, we parents are gods.

To express their criticism of the political establishment, folk-rock musicians of the 1960s wrote protest songs.

Rarely, invert the usual word order to create special effects.

Gone are the days when our children could roam the neighborhood freely.

DESTINATION

For excellent discussion, examples, and exercises on improving sentence variety, visit "Avoiding Primer Language," "The Garden of Phrases," and "Sentence-Combining Skills" at Capital Community Technical College's Guide to Grammar and Writing at <http://ccc.commnet.edu/grammar/>. ■

17 | Consistency and Sentence Logic

"A place for everything, everything in its place."
—BENJAMIN FRANKLIN, writer, scientist, printer

Sentences must make sense. Verbs have to express actions or states of being that the subject is capable of performing or experiencing. Compound structures should be parallel in form, and comparisons must be completed logically. The reader should not be left wondering how the writer intended a sentence to be completed.

EXPRESS!

Consider how simple features of your word processor can help you find illogical or ungrammatical elements in your sentences. For example, save your draft in a new file specifically for sentence editing. To aid you in examining one sentence at a time, create a double space between each sentence. Within a sentence, boldface the subject and the main verb, and then check whether they make sense together. Check items that come in pairs or triplets by arranging the paired elements in a vertical column (see pages 136–137). If you often misplace modifying words such as *only* or *even,* use the "Find" feature to locate each instance for checking. Use all the tools you possess to make sure your sentences make sense.

---

a | Revise Sentence Elements So They Work Together

Logically, the subject must be able to perform the action of the verb, and similarly, words that relate to each other, such as subjects and their complements, must fit together grammatically.

Revise when the subject and predicate don't fit together.

Ellen's **pleasure** in gardening ~~yearned~~ for a bigger yard. *made her yearn*

Pleasure cannot *yearn;* only people can.

The **windows** of the boutique ~~concentrate~~ their attention on suburban hip-hop wannabes.

(attract written above "concentrate"; of written above "on")

Windows cannot *concentrate*.

Revise to make objects and complements match the words to which they are attached.

FAULTY

The kinds of **trips** we love to take are **hunting** and **fishing**.

Hunting and *fishing*, used as nouns, are activities, not trips.

POSSIBLE REVISION

We love to take **hunting and fishing trips**.

FAULTY

These negative attitudes **intimidate** the **enthusiasm** of the volunteers.

Intimidate requires people as its object.

POSSIBLE REVISION

Negative attitudes **undermine** the **enthusiasm** of volunteers.

b Revise the Pattern *something is when*

Common in speech, *something is when* is substandard in written work. Linking verbs such as *is* and *are* act like equations; they signal that the words on each side of the verb are the same kinds of words.

FAULTY

Plagiarism is when you use someone else's work without giving proper credit.

Plagiarism is a noun, so its definition must be another noun or noun equivalent.

POSSIBLE REVISION

Plagiarism is using someone else's work without giving proper credit.

Now *plagiarism* is defined by the noun clause that begins *using someone else's work*.

POSSIBLE REVISION

Plagiarism results when a writer fails to credit a source.

Here *plagiarism* is defined by using an active verb to show a process.

c Revise Tangled Sentences

Sentences sometimes start off in one direction, but then, at a connecting place, seem to "derail" and go in a different direction.

A modifying clause or phrase can cause problems.

OFF TRACK

It is a fact that juveniles, when sent to adult prisons rather than juvenile facilities, two-thirds of them go on to commit more serious crimes.

Lift out the phrase *when sent to adult prisons rather than juvenile facilities* to see that the opening of the sentence doesn't connect with the ending: *It is a fact that juveniles two-thirds of them go on to commit more serious crimes.*

POSSIBLE REVISION

Two-thirds of juveniles, when sent to adult prisons rather than juvenile facilities, go on to commit more serious crimes.

A crucial sentence element may be missing.

INCOMPLETE

If a person is energetic and bright, expecting to do well at our firm.

Here, the opening subordinate clause must eventually connect with an independent clause, but the writer has not supplied one.

POSSIBLE REVISION

If a person is energetic and bright, he or she can expect to do well at our firm.

DERAILED

By writing an excellent legal thriller can make an author a best-seller.

By marks a prepositional phrase. Prepositional phrases cannot function as subjects.

POSSIBLE REVISION

By writing an exciting legal thriller, an author can make the best-seller list.

d Place Modifiers Carefully

Modifiers should be placed near the words they modify. Misplaced modifiers are too far away from the word they modify, causing confusion. Dangling modifiers don't have a word or phrase to modify at all.

Be sure that an introductory modifying phrase is followed directly by the word it modifies, usually the subject of the sentence.

Never having had children, rising college costs ~~do not concern Mirella.~~ *Mirella is unconcerned about*

Supply a word for a dangling modifier to modify.

On returning to the room, *LaTisha found* the furniture had been rearranged.

Place limiting modifiers such as *only, even, almost, nearly,* and *just* immediately before the word they modify.

MISPLACED

Much to his dismay, Hugo realized he had **almost** dated every woman at the party.

Did he date any of the women?

CLARIFIED

Much to his dismay, Hugo realized he had dated **almost** every woman at the party.

When a sentence has more than one verb, make sure it is clear which one the adverb modifies.

MISPLACED

Hearing the guard's footsteps approach **quickly** Mark emptied the safe.

Were the footsteps approaching quickly or did Mark empty the safe quickly?

CLARIFIED

Hearing the guard's footsteps approach, Mark **quickly** emptied the safe.

Note that a comma also helps keep the ideas sorted.

e Add Needed Words

Missing words can derail sentences. Make sure you supply all the words needed to make sentences complete and grammatical.

Add missing words to complete compound structures.

I never have ^(broken) and never will break a promise I make to you.

It costs money both to apply ^(to) and graduate from college.

Without the words added in revision, the sentences are not grammatically correct. Revised, the verb phrase *have broken* parallels the verb phrase *will break*; each consists of a helping verb followed by the appropriate form of the main verb. In the second sentence, *apply to* parallels *graduate from.* Each includes a verb followed by the appropriate preposition.

Add missing words to make comparisons logical.

The programming on cable TV is better suited to young people than ^(that of) the networks.

Two unlike things are compared in the original version: programming and networks.

Juan's responsibilities are greater than ^(those of) the other aides at the hospital.

Responsibilities is illogically compared to *workers.* Adding *those of* compares Juan's responsibilities to theirs.

Add the word *that* if needed to prevent misreading.

Many observers doubt ^(that) the state leaders in the House and Senate are in favor of stronger laws to protect women from abusive domestic partners.

The addition of *that* prevents the reader from thinking that the observers doubt the leaders.

PART FIVE

Sentence Grammar

18 | Repair Sentence Fragments

"I was going to have cosmetic surgery until I noticed the doctor's office was full of portraits by Picasso."
—RITA RUDNER, comic

Sentence fragments are clauses or phrases that look like complete sentences, but either they lack subjects or verbs or they are subordinate constructions. A complete sentence requires at least one independent clause.

> The bill died. **Because the President vetoed it.**

The word *because* changes the independent clause *The President vetoed it* into a subordinate clause, which cannot be presented as a separate sentence.

EXPRESS!

To make sure you catch the fragments in your draft, check every sentence.

1. Does it have a subject-verb pair, with no subordinating word before the pair?
2. Does a verb end in *-ing* or does it follow the word *to*? If so, check to be sure another verb in the sentence is acting as the main verb.
3. Are lists that start with phrases such as *for example* attached to the sentence that precedes them?

This brief check will help you identify many common sentence fragment errors.

To repair sentence fragments (1) attach the fragment to a related sentence or (2) revise the fragment to make it a complete sentence on its own.

a | Clause Fragments

Clause fragments can appear to be complete sentences because they have both a subject and a verb. However, the subordinate words that begin such clauses make them dependent on other ideas for completeness. Subordinating words include *although, be-*

cause, if, since, unless, when, and *while.* Words that begin relative clauses—such as *who, which, that,* and *where*—also signal clauses that must be attached to complete sentences.

It will be a miracle, ~~If~~ *if* the mail comes on time.

When we arrived at the canyon, ~~The~~ *the* sun had already risen.

Roberto was the son of immigrants, ~~W~~*w*ho had never aspired to public office.

Roberto was the son of immigrants. ~~Who~~ *They* had never aspired to public office.

b Phrase Fragments

A phrase fragment lacks a subject, a complete verb, or both. Verbal phrases—phrases with gerunds, participles, or infinitives—are especially tricky because they look like verbs but act as nouns, adjectives, or adverbs. Remember,

- An *-ing* word by itself can never act as the verb of a sentence. It must have an auxiliary verb such as *have, is,* or *were.*
- An infinitive, such as *to run* or *to get,* can never act as the verb of a sentence.

VERBAL FRAGMENTS

Suspecting a coverup, the
~~The~~ reporter asked the senator probing questions. ~~Suspecting a coverup.~~

To create the special effects for *Star Wars,* Industrial Light and Magic was founded by director George Lucas.

An appositive phrase, a word or word group that explains another noun or pronoun, cannot stand alone as a sentence.

The Capitol is on Congress Avenue, ~~The~~ *the* widest street in the city.

c Fragments with Lists

Sometimes a list gets detached from the sentence that introduced or explained it. Lists are often introduced by words or phrases such as *especially, for instance, for example,* and *such as.*

Often you can attach the list to the preceding sentence with a colon or a dash.

> People suffer from many peculiar phobias,~~For~~ ^-for^ example, ailurophobia (fear of cats), aviophobia (fear of flying), and vestiphobia (fear of clothes).

d Intentional Fragments

Intentional fragments are groups of words that convey full ideas even though they may lack subjects, verbs, or both. Intentional fragments enable writers to set a quick pace, present a series of vivid images, or establish a casual tone; they are often used in creating dialogue. You may find intentional fragments in fiction, advertising, and popular magazines.

> Man is the only animal that blushes. Or needs to.
> —Mark Twain

> So what's the best choice? Simple: the PowerCenter 150 from Power Computing.

In any formal or academic writing, fragments should not appear regularly. For readers conservative about grammar, avoid fragments entirely.

DESTINATION

To practice identifying and eliminating fragments, visit The Purdue University OWL at <http://owl.english.purdue.edu/handouts/grammar/g_frag.html>. ■

19 Repair Run-on Sentences

> *"Never express yourself more clearly than you are able to think."*
> —NEILS BOHR, physicist

A comma splice occurs when you try to join two independent clauses with only a comma. A run-on sentence results when no punctuation separates two independent clauses.

COMMA SPLICE

Shawna is an outstanding orator, she has no formal training in speech.

RUN-ON

We were surprised by the package quickly we tore it open.

These errors are serious because they blur the relationship between the independent clauses, but they are easy to identify and fix.

EXPRESS!

Note in each example above that two subject-verb pairs are present.

Shawna is, she has

We were   we tore

As you edit your sentences, search for subject-verb pairs to check whether each pair is separated from the other with a mark stronger than a comma. If only a comma separates them, revise your punctuation.

You have several options for fixing comma splices and run-on sentences.

a Separate Independent Clauses with a Period

Keiko carefully measured the chemicals for the experiment, she ⊙ She
made sure all weights were exact.

b Insert a Semicolon Between Independent Clauses

Use a semicolon when the clauses are closely related.

Marta's entire life revolves around ecological problems she can
speak of little else.

Donald was supposed to be on stage in five minutes, however,
he was still putting on his costume.

Note that when a word such as *however* comes between independent clauses, a semicolon precedes it, and a comma follows it.

c Join Independent Clauses with a Comma and a Coordinating Conjunction

Coordinating conjunctions are *and, or, nor, for, but, yet,* and *so.*

His progress was slow because he did every step by hand, *and* it wasn't easy work.

d Subordinate One Clause to the Other

Albert had to finish the report by himself *because* his irresponsible co-author had lost interest in the cause.

DESTINATION

To learn other strategies for identifying run-ons, visit the Writing Center at the University of North Carolina at Chapel Hill at <http://www.unc.edu/depts/wcweb/handouts/fragments.html>. ∎

20 Make Subjects and Verbs Agree

> *"When I was young, I never wanted to leave the court until I got things exactly correct. My dream was to become a pro."*
>
> —LARRY BIRD, basketball player and coach

Verbs must agree with their subjects in person (*I, you, he, she,* or *it*) and number (singular or plural). With verbs in the present tense, agreement in number is simple: Most subjects take the base form of the verb.

I wait. We wait. You wait. They wait.

The exception to this pattern occurs with third-person singular subjects, such as *he, she, it, the plumber, Ms. Jones.* For these subjects, you must add *-s* or *-es* to the base form.

The plumber waits. She waits.

Ms. Jones goes. He goes.

To choose the correct verb form in the third person, you must know whether the subject is singular or plural. Sometimes it isn't easy to tell.

EXPRESS!

You can find many subject-verb agreement errors by crossing out all the prepositional phrases in a sentence, for example, phrases beginning with *of, in,* and *at.* When you see what words remain, you may find it easier to identify the true subject of the sentence.

Danger ~~of all types continue~~ *continues* to attract people.

You can also cross out all phrases that begin and end with a comma to find the true subject.

All politicians, ~~regardless of their ideology, embraces~~ *embrace* the goal that every child should be able to read by the end of third grade.

These two simple steps will help you catch many typical agreement errors.

---

a Words Between Subject and Verb

When subjects and verbs are separated by other word groups, make sure the verb agrees with the subject and not another noun that falls in between.

The numerous dams in the river ~~was~~ *were* built by beavers.

Phrases such as *along with, as well as,* or *together with* do not make a singular subject plural.

The National Weather Service, as well as many police officers, ~~wish~~ *wishes* amateurs wouldn't chase severe storms.

When a singular verb sounds awkward, consider joining the subjects with *and* instead.

b Subjects Joined by *and*

Subjects joined by *and* are usually plural.

Hail and a rotating cloud wall ~~indicate~~ *indicates* the possibility of a tornado.

Exceptions: Treat the compound subject as singular if

- the two parts of the subject describe a single idea: *Peace and quiet **is** rare. Rock and roll **is** here to stay.*
- the subject is preceded by *every* or *each*: *Each spring and each fall **brings** the danger of more clouds. Every storm chaser and newsperson **wants** great pictures of the storm.*

c Subjects Joined by *or* or *nor*

The verb, or its auxiliary, agrees in number with the subject nearer to the verb.

Heavy rain or baseball-sized hail ~~cause~~ *causes* the most damage.

Either severe lightning or powerful bouts of hail ~~is~~ *are* apt to accompany the development of a supercell.

d Indefinite Pronouns Such as *anyone*

Indefinite pronouns are pronouns that do not refer to a particular person, thing, or group. In formal writing, treat the following indefinite pronouns as singular: *anybody, anyone, anything, everybody, everyone, everything, nobody, no one, nothing, somebody, someone, something, each.*

Each **believes** decisive action needs to be taken.

Some indefinite pronouns vary in whether they refer to an individual or a group: *all, any, either, more, most, neither, none, some.* Use the singular or plural depending on the meaning you intend.

Most of this apple **is** rotten.

Most of the voters **favor** the legislation.

Few, many, and *several* are always plural.

e Collective Nouns Such as *team*

Collective nouns name a group: *team, choir, band, orchestra, jury, committee, faculty, family.* Usually, collective nouns emphasize the group as a unit, and they take singular verbs. However, they sometimes refer to separate individuals or parts of the group, and in this case, they take plural verbs.

SINGULAR

The jury **expects** its verdict to be controversial.

PLURAL

The jury **agree** not to discuss their verdict with the press.

Usually your writing will be smoother if you treat collective nouns as singular subjects.

Note: Measurements are singular as a unit but plural as individual components.

Six months **is** the waiting period.

Six months **have** passed.

f Subject After Verb

A verb agrees with its subject, no matter where the subject appears in the sentence.

Was their motive to get revenge?

Among those requesting Chief Harley's resignation **were** many citizens.

Here **is** a surprising turn of events.

g *Who, which,* and *that* as Subjects

The relative pronouns *who, which,* and *that* refer to antecedents, just as other pronouns do. When a relative pronoun is used as a subject, the verb agrees with the antecedent.

The killer whale is a mammal that **demonstrates** highly complex social behavior.

A subtle agreement problem occurs with the phrase *one of the.* In general, use a plural verb form with *one of the,* but use a singular verb form when you add *only* to the phrase: *only one of the.*

seem
Ransom is one of the city officials who always seems enthusiastic.

Some officials always seem enthusiastic, and Ransom is one of them. *Who* refers to *city officials,* and the verb is plural.

Ransom is the only one of the city officials who always ~~seem~~ *seems*
enthusiastic.

Only one city official always seems enthusiastic—Ransom. *Who*
refers to *one,* and the verb is singular.

h   Linking Verbs and Complements

Common linking verbs are *to be, to seem, to appear, to feel, to
taste, to look,* and *to become.* A linking verb agrees with its subject,
which usually precedes the verb, not with the subject complement, which follows it.

The key to a candidate's success ~~are~~ *is* television appearances.

The subject is *key,* not *appearances.*

i   Plural Forms, Singular Meanings

Some words that end in *-s* are singular in meaning and take
singular verbs: *physics, statistics, mathematics, measles, mumps, news.*
Consult a dictionary if you are unsure whether a word is singular
or plural.

Mathematics ~~are~~ *is* perceived as a difficult subject by many
students.

Other singular terms—*series, segment, portion, fragment,
part*—usually remain singular even when modified by plural
words.

A series of questions ~~are~~ *is* posed by a reporter.

The word *majority* can function as both a singular and a plural noun.

SINGULAR   The majority **rules.**

PLURAL   The majority of critics **want** the police chief to
be fired.

j Titles and Words Used as Words

Titles and words referred to as words always take singular verbs, even when their own forms are plural.

The Adventures of Rocky and Bullwinkle stars~~star~~ Rene Russo as Natasha Fatale and Jason Alexander as Boris Badenov.

The word *physics* comes~~come~~ from the Latin "physica," meaning "natural science."

DESTINATION

For a basic review of subjects and predicates, visit "HyperGrammar" at the University of Ottawa at <http://www.uottawa.ca/academic/arts/writcent/hypergrammar/subjpred.html>. ■

21 Check Verbs

"Any activity becomes creative when the doer cares about doing it right, or doing it better."
—JOHN UPDIKE, novelist

Verbs express actions and states of being: *run, exist.* They express the time or time frame in which actions occur—the past, present, future—and relations among events that happen at different times. Verbs also vary in form: Not all verbs form the past tense or past participles in a regular, consistent way. Verbs show whether a writer intends to make a statement, a command, or more subtly, a wish, a hope, or a suggestion. Using the correct verb form requires close attention.

EXPRESS!

When editing verbs, first check an entire passage—a paragraph or group of related paragraphs—to discover whether you have established a dominant time frame for the passage. Do most of the verbs

(continued)

Express! (continued)

express current actions, for example? If not, read the passage carefully to decide on your main purpose. Are you describing something you want your readers to feel is happening now? If so, consider changing many of the verbs to the present tense. Are you recounting a past incident? Are you speculating about the future? Not all verbs have to be in a single tense. But unless you establish a dominant time frame, you are likely to confuse your readers.

a   Regular and Irregular Verbs

Regular verbs form both the past tense and the past participle by adding *-d* or *-ed* to the base form of the verb: *advertise, advertised, advertised; talk, talked, talked.* Irregular verbs do not follow this pattern, however; they change their forms in various ways.

Consult a dictionary or the following list to be sure you're using the correct verb form. The list gives the three principal parts of each verb: the base form, or present tense; the simple past tense; and the past participle. The past participle is used with auxiliary verbs to form verb phrases such as *I have ridden, I had ridden, I will have ridden.*

Irregular Verbs

Present	Past	Past Participle
arise	arose	arisen
bear (carry)	bore	borne
bear (give birth)	bore	borne, born
become	became	become
begin	began	begun
bite	bit	bitten, bit
blow	blew	blown
break	broke	broken
bring	brought	brought
burst	burst	burst
buy	bought	bought
catch	caught	caught
choose	chose	chosen
cling	clung	clung
come	came	come
creep	crept	crept

Present	Past	Past Participle
dig	dug	dug
dive	dived, dove	dived
do	did	done
draw	drew	drawn
dream	dreamed, dreamt	dreamed, dreamt
drink	drank	drunk
drive	drove	driven
eat	ate	eaten
fall	fell	fallen
find	found	found
fly	flew	flown
forget	forgot	forgotten
forgive	forgave	forgiven
freeze	froze	frozen
get	got	got, gotten
give	gave	given
go	went	gone
grow	grew	grown
hang (an object)	hung	hung
hang (a person)	hanged, hung	hanged, hung
know	knew	known
lay (to place)	laid	laid
lead	led	led
leave	left	left
lend	lent	lent
lie (to recline)	lay	lain
light	lit, lighted	lit, lighted
lose	lost	lost
pay	paid	paid
plead	pleaded, pled	pleaded, pled
prove	proved	proved, proven
ride	rode	ridden
ring	rang, rung	rung
rise	rose	risen
run	ran	run
say	said	said
see	saw	seen
set	set	set
shake	shook	shaken
shine	shone, shined	shone, shined
show	showed	shown, showed

(continued)

Irregular Verbs (continued)

Present	Past	Past Participle
shrink	shrank, shrunk	shrunk
sing	sang, sung	sung
sink	sank, sunk	sunk
sit	sat	sat
speak	spoke	spoken
spring	sprang, sprung	sprung
stand	stood	stood
steal	stole	stolen
sting	stung	stung
swear	swore	sworn
swim	swam	swum
swing	swung	swung
take	took	taken
tear	tore	torn
throw	threw	thrown
wake	woke, waked	woken, waked
wear	wore	worn
wring	wrung	wrung
write	wrote	written

b *Lie* and *lay, sit* and *set, rise* and *raise*

These three pairs of verbs cause much confusion. *Lay, set,* and *raise* are all transitive verbs—they take direct objects. *Lay* means to "to place" or "to put"; *set* also means "to place" or "to put"; *raise* means "to lift up." These verbs require direct objects to complete their meanings.

Jenny lays a book on her desk. (*book* is the direct object)

Then she sets her plate on the nearby table. (*plate* is the direct object)

All this so her mother won't raise her voice in protest. (*voice* is the direct object)

Lie, sit, and *rise* are intransitive; they don't take objects. *Lie* means "to recline"; *sit* means "to take a seat"; and *rise* means "to get up."

Travis lies under the cottonwood tree.

He sits near the fountain to avoid the shade.

Then he rises and walks slowly away.

Consult this table to be sure you use the correct forms of these troublesome verbs.

Base Form	Present -s Form	Past	Present Participle	Past Participle
lie (recline)	lies	lay	lying	lain
lay (put)	lays	laid	laying	laid
sit (be seated)	sits	sat	sitting	sat
set (put)	sets	set	setting	set
rise (get up)	rises	rose	rising	risen
raise (lift)	raises	raised	raising	raised

c Verb Tenses

Verb tense reveals when an action is taking place. English has three simple tenses—the present, past, and future. The present tense is used for actions occurring in the present and for actions that occur regularly. The past tense describes actions completed in the past. The future tense describes actions that will occur in the future.

PRESENT   I answer the question. I always answer.

PAST   I answered quickly.

FUTURE   I will answer the phone tomorrow.

The perfect forms of each tense (a form of *have* + the past participle) describe actions that were or will be completed by the time of another action.

PRESENT PERFECT   I have answered that question before.

PAST PERFECT   I had answered just before the alarm sounded.

FUTURE PERFECT   I will have answered the questions by Monday.

The progressive forms of each tense (a form of *be* + the present participle) express continuing actions.

PRESENT PROGRESSIVE   I am answering now.

PAST PROGRESSIVE   I was answering when the lights went out.

FUTURE PROGRESSIVE   I will be answering the phones all day.

The perfect progressive forms of each tense (a form of *have* + a form of *be* + the present participle) combine to express more complex time relationships.

PRESENT PERFECT PROGRESSIVE	I have been answering your questions.
PAST PERFECT PROGRESSIVE	I had been answering before you interrupted.
FUTURE PERFECT PROGRESSIVE	I will have been answering for nine hours by the time you arrive at midnight.

Use present tense for special purposes.
Use the present tense to introduce quotations and refer to actions in literary works.

The doctor in *Macbeth* ~~warned~~ ^{warns} a gentlewoman, "You know what you should not" (5.1.46–47).

Use the present tense to express a general statement of fact or a scientific truth.

Einstein ~~argued~~ ^{argues} that the principle of relativity ~~applied~~ ^{applies} to all physical phenomena.

Use past perfect tense appropriately.
The past perfect tense allows you to show exactly how one event in the past stands in relation to another event in time. Use it to make your writing more precise.

Audrey could not believe that Kyle ^{had} actually asked her to pay for his lunch.

Be consistent.
Establish a dominant time frame in your writing and stick with it. Don't shift tenses needlessly; use different tenses to indicate shifts in time.

The lawyer had already explained the options to her client and was waiting for his decision.

DESTINATION

For more examples of using tense shifts appropriately, and for practice in revising unnecessary tense shifts, visit the Online Writing Lab at Purdue University at <http://owl.english.purdue.edu/handouts/grammar/g_tensec.html>. ■

d Active and Passive Voice

Verbs that take objects (transitive verbs) can be in the active or passive voice. Voice indicates whether the subject of a sentence acts or is acted upon. In active voice, subjects perform actions; in passive voice, the action is done *to* the subject.

ACTIVE   Mr. Yeh **managed** the advertising campaign.

PASSIVE   The advertising campaign **was managed** by Mr. Yeh.

Many writers prefer active sentences because they are simple, direct, and easy to read; they keep prose lively. If you want to change a sentence from passive voice to active voice, make the performer of the action the subject of the sentence or clause.

Management approved the   *the engineering staff completed*
~~The~~ designs ~~were approved by management~~ before ˄ work on them ~~was completed by the engineering staff.~~

Not every passive verb should be made active. The passive voice is useful, for example, when the action is more important than who performed it, or when you simply don't know who performed an action.

Dozens were arrested at the concert.

The van was stolen.

DESTINATION

Science, medical, and legal fields use the passive voice regularly; for a complete explanation of how to change a sentence from active to passive voice, visit "Guide to Grammar & Writing" at <http://webster.commnet.edu/grammar/passive.htm>. ■

e The Subjunctive Mood

Mood indicates how a writer intends a statement to be taken. If the writer is making a direct statement or asking a question, the mood is indicative. If the writer gives a command, the mood is imperative. The subjunctive mood is a bit more subtle. It is used to express a wish or a hope, make a suggestion, or speculate about how a situation might be. In most cases, you need only change a *was* to a *were* to mark the subjunctive mood.

If Jimail ~~was~~ *were* in charge, we would be in good hands.

If she ~~was~~ *were* to accept their terms, she could sign the contract.

Notice that the subjunctive verb is in the *if* clause, and the modal auxiliaries *would* and *could* are in the other clause.

For all verbs, the present subjunctive is the base form of the verb—*be, give, bless.* This is true even in the third person singular, where you might expect a different form.

The officer asked that everyone ~~is~~ *be* silent.

It is essential that *Emily* ~~has~~ *have* her lines memorized by tomorrow.

For all verbs except *be,* the past subjunctive is the same as the simple past tense—*gave, blessed, sent.* For *be,* the past subjunctive is always *were.*

---

22 Check Pronouns

"You'll always miss 100% of the shots you don't take."
　　　　　　　—WAYNE GRETSKY, hockey player

Pronouns stand in for nouns and act like nouns, but they don't name a specific person, place, or thing—*I, you, he, she, it, we, they, whom, this, that, one,* and *which,* for example. A pronoun should clearly refer to its noun to avoid confusion (pronoun reference). A pronoun should match its noun in person, number, and gender (pronoun agreement). A pronoun's form should match its function in a sentence (pronoun case).

Workers denied that **they** intended to strike.

The pronoun *they* clearly refers back to its noun, *workers.* The pronoun also agrees with the noun: Both are plural in number and subjective in case.

EXPRESS!

Pronouns alter the distance between you and your readers. Choosing *I, we,* or *you* puts you closer to readers; using *one* creates more distance. Take responsibility with *I* or *we,* speak directly to readers with *you,* and consider using *one* to convey a general truth or moral sentiment. Whether your writing situation calls for familiarity or distance, don't switch pronoun forms in the middle of a sentence or paragraph. Maintain a reasonable consistency for your readers' sake.

a Pronoun Reference

The noun a pronoun refers to is called its *antecedent.* The antecedent is the word you'd have to repeat in a sentence if you couldn't use a pronoun—*workers* in the example above.

Revise ambiguous references. When a pronoun could refer to two possible antecedents, revise the sentence.

> When they talked ~~Jackie talked to Andrea that~~ at noon, ~~she~~ Jackie did not realize that ~~she~~ Andrea might be resigning before the end of the day.

Because both Jackie and Andrea are female, the pronoun *she* in the original sentence could refer to either of them.

Check *this, that, which,* and *it*. Pronouns must refer to specific antecedents. Pronouns can't refer to a group of words or to a vague idea. Replace the pronoun with a noun, add a specific antecedent, or change other wording to make your reference clear.

> The novel is filled with violence, brutality, and refined language. I especially like this~~.~~ combination of toughness and grace.

> The house has a tiny kitchen, which the owners intend to remodel, and a dilapidated porch. ~~, which the owners intend to remodel~~.

> While nuclear waste products are hard to dispose of safely, ~~it~~ nuclear power remains a reasonable alternative to burning fossil fuels to produce electricity.

Check to be sure the antecedent is stated. Pronouns can't refer to antecedents that are merely implied in the sentence.

Be especially careful to check for a stated antecedent when the pronoun is *they* or *it*.

In Houston, ~~they~~ _people_ live more casually than in Dallas.

~~In the~~ _The_ paper, ~~it~~ said that we should pass new school bonds.

Make sure the antecedent is not a possessive form.

Possessive nouns—such as *expert's, children's, Smiths'*—cannot be used as antecedents.

As for the ~~experts' view of the Miata~~ _experts_, they either praise _the Miata_ ~~it~~ or wish it had more power.

DESTINATION

For more discussion and examples of pronoun reference, as well as practices, visit *HyperGrammar* at the University of Ottawa at
<http://www.uottawa.ca/academic/arts/writcent/hypergrammar/pronref.html>.

b   Pronoun Agreement

Pronouns and nouns are either singular or plural. Make sure the pronoun matches the noun: Singular pronouns go with singular nouns, and plural pronouns go with plural nouns.

A victorious quarterback always enjoys hearing hometown crowds cheering in the stands for ~~them~~ _him_.

Check pronouns that refer to collective nouns.   Collective nouns describe groups or collections of things: *class, team, band, orchestra, jury, committee, audience, family, Congress.* Usually, collective nouns refer to a group as a single unit, so pronouns that refer to collective nouns are usually singular. If you use a collective noun to refer to individual members of a group, however, then the noun is plural and the pronoun must also be plural.

The jury rendered ~~their~~ _its_ decision.

The chorus took ~~its~~ _their_ seats.

In most cases, sentences sound more natural if you treat collective nouns as singular. You can always add the word *members* before a collective noun when you are referring to individuals. *Members* becomes the antecedent, and the pronoun is plural.

The *members* of the chorus took **their** seats.

Check pronouns that refer to indefinite pronouns.
First, decide whether an indefinite pronoun is singular or plural.

ALWAYS SINGULAR

anybody, anyone, anything, each, everybody, everyone, everything, nobody, no one, nothing, somebody, someone, something

ALWAYS PLURAL

few, many, several

Then make sure the pronoun matches the indefinite pronoun in number.

Everyone is entitled to ~~their~~ *his or her* opinion.

Each of the legislators had ~~their~~ *his or her* say.

Some indefinite pronouns can be either singular or plural, depending on how you use them. These pronouns are *all, any, either, more, most, neither, none,* and *some.* Sometimes, words modifying the pronoun may determine the number.

All of the portraits had yellowed in **their** frames.

All of the wine is still in **its** casks.

None is considered variable because it is often accepted as a plural form. However, in formal writing, *none* is usually treated as singular.

None of the churches had **its** doors locked.

Check antecedents joined by *or* and *nor.*
When two singular antecedents are joined by *or, nor, either . . . or,* or *neither . . . nor,* refer to them with a singular pronoun.

Neither Brazil nor Mexico will raise ~~their~~ *its* oil prices today.

When two plural antecedents are joined by these words, use plural pronouns to refer to them.

Either the players or the managers will file **their** grievances.

When a singular noun is joined to a plural noun by these words, the pronoun should agree with the nearer noun in number and in gender.

Either the stress-filled hours in the office or a poor diet will
take ~~their~~ its toll on the business executive.

DESTINATION

For detailed examples of how to correct basic problems of pronoun agreement, visit The Write Place at St. Cloud State University at <http://leo.stcloudstate.edu/grammar/pronante.html>. ■

c Pronoun Case

The personal pronouns and the pronoun *who* change in
form—or case—according to their function in a sentence. Pronouns used as subjects or subject complements take the subjective
case; pronouns used as objects take the objective case; and pronouns used as possessives take the possessive case.

Subjective Case	Objective Case	Possessive Case
I	me	my, mine
we	us	our, ours
you	you	your, yours
he	him	his
she	her	her, hers
it	it	its, of it
they	them	their, theirs
who	whom	whose

In most cases, writers automatically select the right form. But in a
few situations, choosing between *I* and *me, he* or *him,* or *who* and
whom can be tricky.

DESTINATION

To review pronoun case, visit the *Writer's Workshop* at <http://
www.english.uiuc.edu/cws/wworkshop/grammar/case.htm>. ■

Check pairs of pronouns.   The second pronoun in a pair is
often troublesome. If you take out the first pronoun, you'll often
be able to tell immediately which case to use for the second one.

Similarly, in a noun-pronoun pair, take out the noun and examine what's left.

> _I_
> You and ~~me~~ don't have the latest designs yet.

You would never say "Me don't."

> _her_
> The memo praised you and ~~she~~.

You wouldn't say "praised she."

> _me_
> The flowers are for Elena and ~~I~~.

"For I"?

Check pronouns after linking verbs. Linking verbs, such as _to be, to seem, to appear, to feel,_ and _to become,_ connect a subject to a word or phrase that completes or extends its meaning—the subject complement. In formal writing, use the subjective case for the subject complement.

> _I_
> It is ~~me~~.

> _who_
> You are ~~whom~~?

> _she_
> The next CEO will be ~~her~~.

Check _we_ or _us_ when they are followed by nouns. The pronoun and following noun must share the same case. Take away the noun to check the case of the pronoun.

> _We_
> ~~Us~~ lucky sailors missed the storm.

"Us missed"?

> _us_
> For ~~we~~ engineers, the job market looks promising.

"For we"?

Check pronouns in comparisons. To determine pronoun case after _than, like,_ or _as,_ complete the comparison.

> _he_
> I am taller than ~~him~~.

I am taller than him is?

> _she_
> We don't invest as much as ~~her~~.

We don't invest as much as her does?

When the comparison could be completed either way, the pronoun you select will determine the meaning of the sentence. To avoid possible confusion, you can always write out the full comparison.

> Rodeos do not interest me as much as she. (as much as she interests me)

> Rodeos do not interest me as much as her. (as much as they interest her)

Check who and whom.   The subjective form—*who* or *whoever*—is used when a pronoun is a subject or a subject complement. The objective form—*whom* or *whomever*—is used when a pronoun is an object.

> *who*
> ~~Whom~~ wrote this letter?

Who is the subject.

> *whom*
> You addressed who?

Whom is the object of the verb *addressed.*

> *whom*
> To who did you write?

Whom is the object of the preposition *to.*

When the pronoun is part of a subordinate clause, isolate the clause. Decide which case to use based on the pronoun's function in the clause, not in the whole sentence.

> ┌─ subordinate clause ─┐
> The system rewards whoever works hard.

Whoever is the subject of the clause *whoever works hard.* It has its own verb, *works.* Thus it is in the subjective case.

> ┌─ subordinate clause ─┐
> Juanita told her parents she would marry whomever she wanted.

In the clause *whomever she wanted,* the subject is *she,* the verb is *wanted,* and the object is *whomever.*

Check pronouns in appositives.   Appositives are nouns or phrases that restate or add information to a previous noun. When an appositive contains a pronoun, the pronoun should be in the same case as the noun it modifies.

> *me*
> The instructor called two students, Sara and I, to her office.

Two students, the noun phrase being modified, is the object of the verb *called.* So the pronoun should be in the objective case.

d Nonsexist Pronoun Use

What should you do when you need to use a pronoun, but don't know whether it should refer to a man or a woman?

Each of the editors walked to (his? her?) car.

Until a few years ago, most writers would use a masculine pronoun (*he, him, his*) in such a situation. However, this usage is sexist, because it implies that a particular group (of editors, pilots, engineers, senators, or students, for example) would not include any women. Similarly, in the following sentence, the implication is that only women are nurses.

> SEXIST   An experienced nurse knows when her patient
>   needs extra care.

Clearly, even if this were true before, it is not true today—truck drivers, teachers, students, and secretaries can be men or women. (Obviously, you should acknowledge the inevitable exceptions: *Each of the nuns received an award for **her** assistance.*) Be sure that your language accommodates both sexes.

Use the expressions *he or she, him or her,* or *his or her.*

Every secretary may invite ~~her husband.~~ his or her spouse

However, *he or she* expressions quickly become tiresome. If you have more than one such expression in a sentence, consider your other choices.

Change a singular reference to a plural one.

Before ~~he or she~~ leaves, ~~each~~ all member~~s~~ of the band should be
sure ~~he or she has his or her~~ they have their music.

Delete the pronoun altogether.

Nobody should leave ~~until he has signed~~ without signing the guest book.

For some readers, use a plural pronoun with indefi-nite pronouns formerly considered singular. Although this pronoun-referent *dis*agreement—very common in speech—is gaining limited acceptance in writing, be warned that many readers still consider such forms simply wrong.

Every skier took his turn on the ski slopes. *(their)*

If you keep searching for the best way to make your language inclusive, you'll often find an excellent solution.

Every skier took his turn on the ski slopes. *(a)*

Note that expressions such as *he/she, s/he,* and *s'he* are not widely accepted.

e Other Pronoun Problems

Two other problems writers sometimes have with pronouns are deciding when to use an apostrophe in the word *its* and knowing when to use *that, which,* and *who* in modifiers.

Its/it's **and** *whose/who's.* It is easy to confuse the possessive pronoun *its,* which has no apostrophe, with the contraction for *it is—it's*—which does include an apostrophe. The possessive forms of a personal pronoun never take an apostrophe, while contractions always require one.

The van lost it's hubcaps while parked on the street. *(its)*

Its a shame that thefts in the neighborhood have increased. *(It's)*

If you consistently misuse *its/it's,* try reading *it's* as *it is* when checking your work. Eventually you will eliminate this error.

Similarly, *whose* is a possessive pronoun; *who's* is the contraction for *who is* or *who was.*

Who's teammate is on first base? *(whose)*

Whose on first? *(Who's)*

That, which, **and** *who.* These words require special attention when they serve as relative pronouns introducing modifying clauses. Restrictive (essential) clauses are essential to understanding the terms they modify or explain. Restrictive clauses are not enclosed by commas and are often introduced by *that*.

The report ***that** I wrote* recommended the sale.

In contrast, the information in a nonrestrictive clause is important, but not essential to the meaning of the sentence. When a nonrestrictive clause is deleted, the sentence still makes sense. Nonrestrictive clauses are enclosed by commas and introduced by *which*.

The report, ***which** the team dashed off at the last minute,* recommended profit sharing.

Try removing the modifying clauses beginning with *that, which,* or *who*. Does the sentence still make sense, or will the reader be left with further questions? If the sentence still makes sense without the clause, then the clause is probably nonrestrictive and is enclosed by commas. If essential meaning is lost without the clause, then it is restrictive and is not enclosed by commas.

The popularity ***that** Charlie Chaplin enjoyed* during the early days of film may never be equaled.

Without the modifying clause, the sentence reads: *The popularity during the early days of film may never be equaled.* Essential meaning is lost; thus, the clause is restrictive and is not enclosed by commas.

His graceful gestures and matchless acrobatics, ***which** some critics likened to ballet,* were perfectly suited to the silent screen.

Without the modifying clause, the sentence reads: *His graceful gestures and matchless acrobatics were perfectly suited to the silent screen.* While the clause adds interesting additional detail, it is not essential to the main thought. Thus the clause is nonrestrictive and is enclosed by commas.

The meaning you intend will often determine whether a modifying clause should be enclosed by commas.

The car that hit me rolled into the ditch.

Because no commas are used around *that hit me,* the sentence implies that several cars are involved, and the one that hit the writer, not one of the others, is the one that rolled into the ditch.

The car, which hit me, rolled into the ditch.

Now there's only one car, one that readers already know about. That it hit the writer is incidental information in a larger discussion about the car.

Finally, always use *who* rather than *that* or *which* to refer to a human subject:

The woman ~~that~~ who waved was my boss.

23 Check Adjectives and Adverbs

"Never be afraid to sit awhile and think."
—LORRAINE HANSBERRY, playwright

Adjectives and adverbs carry important information, giving your reader specific details about other words in the sentence. Using the standard forms of adjectives and adverbs lends you credibility as a writer.

ADJECTIVES	A **successful** mayor is **rare** these days.
	Tall and **redheaded**, he looked **Irish**.
ADVERBS	The water was **extremely** cold.
	Richard plays **fair**.

If you need help in placing adjectives, adverbs, and other modifiers, see 17d.

EXPRESS!

Add interest to your writing by varying your use of modifiers—adjectives, adverbs, phrases, and clauses. Consider how you can add layers of detail so that readers will not only understand your point but also enjoy reading about it. For example, in the following sentence, notice how the writer uses a variety of strategies to describe his subject.

Farmer is an inch or two over six feet and thin, unusually long-legged and long-armed, and he has an agile way of folding himself into a chair and arranging himself around a patient he is examining that made me think of a grasshopper.

—Tracy Kidder, "The Good Doctor"

a Adjectives

Adjectives modify nouns or pronouns; they answer the questions *which? how many?* and *what kind?*

Check for adjective pileups. Most, but not all, adjectives come before the nouns or pronouns they modify. You can add variety and interest by placing some adjectives after the words they modify. Revise your sentence when so many adjectives are strung together that readers will become confused or bored.

CONFUSING	Adam had his ~~enthusiastic~~ parents' support. *(enthusiastic)*
TEDIOUS	Our confident, ~~stylish, and experienced~~ marching band won a national title. *(, stylish and experienced,)*

Check words after linking verbs. Use adjectives—not adverbs—after linking verbs such as *seem, become, look, appear, feel,* and *smell.* These predicate adjectives give information about the subject of the sentence; they modify a noun or pronoun.

I feel badly. *(good)*

Lillian acts optimistically about her chances for getting into the graduate program. *(optimistic)*

Remember that some verbs can be used as both linking verbs and action verbs. If the verb describes an action rather than a state of being, use an adverb to modify the verb.

Wet dogs smell badly. (adjective after linking verb) *(good)*

The dog smells rotting leaves excited. (adverb after action verb) *(excitedly)*

Check *good* and *well*. *Good* is always an adjective. Use *good* after a linking verb when you want to give information about the subject.

Jasper Hayes looks **good**.

When you are referring to someone's health, use *well* after the linking verb.

Most college students feel **well** in spite of their poor eating habits.

Don't use *good* as an adverb. Use *well* to modify verbs.

Most jobs in child care don't pay **well**.

Don't qualify absolute adjectives.
Some adjectives express an absolute, something that cannot be compared or modified: *perfect, unique, singular, empty, equal, absolute, pregnant.* Don't use qualifiers (such as *less, more, most, least, very*) with these absolute adjectives.

Jack's story is ~~more~~ unique~~than~~ Jane's~~.~~ ; *is not*

Janice thought the software program was ~~absolutely~~ perfect.

DESTINATION

Nonnative speakers may find helpful the pages on "Grammar When You Need It," "Position of Adjectives," and, especially, "Order of Adjectives" at <http://www.geocities.com:0080/Athens/Olympus/7583/adjposition.html>. ∎

b Adverbs

Adverbs modify verbs, adjectives, or other adverbs, answering the questions *where? when?* and *how?* Many adverbs end in *-ly*: *The investment broker spoke **evasively**.* But some adverbs have both short and long forms: *quick/quickly.*

Use the -ly form in formal writing situations.
For most academic and business audiences, you'll do better to use the long, *-ly* form. In more casual and colloquial writing, you can use the short forms.

STANDARD	We drive **slowly** in town.
COLLOQUIAL	Connie drives **slow**.
STANDARD	The employees asked to be treated **fairly**.
COLLOQUIAL	The employees asked to be treated **fair**.

Watch for double negatives.
Using two *no* words—*no, not, nothing, nobody, never*—in the same sentence or independent

clause is considered nonstandard. When you find you've used two of these words, usually you can just drop or change a single word.

> That parrot ~~doesn't~~ never talk. ^s

> John doesn't want ~~no~~ help. ^any

Similarly, don't mix the negative adverbs *hardly, scarcely,* or *barely* with another negative word or phrase.

> The morning was so clear that the hikers ~~couldn't~~ hardly wait to get started. ^could

However, to express an idea positively but with some reservation, you may use two negatives.

> Sean was hardly unattractive.

c Comparatives and Superlatives

Adjectives and adverbs both have comparative forms and superlative forms. The comparative and superlative forms of most adjectives and adverbs can be expressed two ways.

ugly (an adjective)

COMPARATIVE	uglier	more ugly
SUPERLATIVE	ugliest	most ugly

slowly (an adverb)

COMPARATIVE	slower	more slowly
SUPERLATIVE	slowest	most slowly

Generally, add *-er* and *-est* endings to one-syllable adjectives and adverbs, but use the terms *more* and *most, less* and *least* before words of two or more syllables.

> Camille talks **faster** than Susi.

> Susi usually speaks **more deliberately**.

Use the comparative to compare two items.

> Juan was the ~~smartest~~ of the two children. ^smarter

> Celeste, his twin, was the ~~most~~ imaginative. ^more

Use the superlative to compare three or more items.

Given the choice of several toys, Celeste would choose the
most
~~more~~ challenging one.
∧

Don't use double forms.　Use only one form in a phrase.

Jasper was ~~more~~ stricter as a parent than Janice was.

Of the whole archery team, Diana was the ~~most~~ angriest about
the stolen targets.

PART SIX

Grammar for ESL Writers

If you speak English as a second language, you may want to review Chapters 24–26 for strategies to find and correct common grammatical errors. In these chapters you will also find references to other sources of information—books, Web sites, and other sections of this handbook—that we recommend you consult for in-depth help with writing and grammar. Both ESL and native speakers of English may want to use Chapter 26, Proofreading in English, as a checklist for editing. ■

24 | Nouns, Articles, and Quantifiers

"Not everything that can be counted counts, and not everything that counts can be counted."
—ALBERT EINSTEIN, physicist

Do you ever need help figuring out which article to use—*a, an,* or *the?* Do you know when no article should be used? Are you sometimes uncertain about whether to use *a few* or *a little* before some nouns? If so, this chapter will help you distinguish between count and noncount nouns, and the articles and quantifiers that go with them.

EXPRESS!

When deciding whether to use a definite or indefinite article before a noun, ask yourself the following questions.

- Have I mentioned the noun before?
- Does the situation make the noun's specific identity clear?
- Have I used a phrase or clause after the noun that makes it specific?

If your response to any of these questions is "yes," and if you can also make the noun plural, you can probably use the definite article *the* before the noun.

---

a | Count and Noncount Nouns

Nouns in English are either count nouns or noncount nouns. Count nouns are items that you can count or things that you can divide easily: *six books, sixty minutes.* Noncount nouns refer to things or ideas that cannot be counted or divided: *air, love, chemistry.*

Count nouns are singular (*finger*) or plural (*fingers*). Noncount nouns usually have only a single form: *gasoline.* You can often give a noncount noun a count meaning by adding a phrase such as *an instance of, a serving of,* or *a type of* before the noncount noun. In conversation, native speakers may omit the phrase, which can be confusing.

May we have three **waters**, please? (informal speech)

May we have three **glasses of water**, please? (full meaning)

Since you can't count noncount nouns, you can't use numbers or other expressions (*many, several*) that indicate numbers with noncount nouns.

Examples of noncount nouns

Mass nouns: air, gasoline, plastic, rain, wood, wool

Food and drink: cheese, chocolate, coffee, fish, meat, milk, rice, tea, water

Abstract nouns: advice, beauty, employment, information, knowledge, satisfaction

Others: clothing, furniture, hair, homework, money, news, traffic, work

When you are unsure whether a noun is count or noncount, consult an ESL dictionary. See page 188 for a recommendation.

b Definite and Indefinite Articles

The or *a/an* with a singular count noun.   With a singular count noun, you need an article. As a rule, use the definite article when it is clear which specific thing you are referring to, and the indefinite article when the reader or listener cannot be expected to know which particular item you mean.

1. Use the indefinite article *a* or *an* when you introduce the noun for the first time, and once your reader understands the reference, use the definite article *the*.

   There are several reasons why a person may end up homeless. Perhaps the person lost his or her job and could not pay for an apartment. Or perhaps the apartment was sold to a new owner who raised the rent. The new owner may not realize how expensive the rent is for that person.

2. Use *the* when the noun is specified by a phrase or clause that follows it.

   The book
   ~~Book~~ that I read is informative.

   The
   ~~A~~ book **on Robert Kennedy** is out.

3. Use *the* with the superlative adjective.

the
This is ⌃best brand you can buy.

4. Use *the* when the context makes it clear which specific thing is being referred to.

The earth
⌃Earth is round. (There is only one earth.)

the
Please take ⌃a cake out of the oven. (Both speaker and listener know which cake.)

5. When making generalizations, you can use *a/an* or *the* with most singular count nouns.

A dog can be good company for **a** lonely **person**. (any dog; any lonely person)

The computer has changed the banking industry dramatically. (the computer in general)

The capitalist believes in free enterprise. (*The* is used to make general statements about specific species of animals or groups of people—e.g., capitalists.)

Use no article to make general statements with plural count nouns and noncount nouns.

Computers
~~The computers~~ have changed the banking industry dramatically. (plural count noun)

Sugar
~~The sugar~~ is a major cause of tooth decay. (noncount noun)

c Quantifiers

The words that come before nouns and tell you *how much* or *how many* are called *quantifiers*. Quantifiers are not always the same for both count and noncount nouns.

- *Use with count and noncount nouns:* some, a lot of, plenty of, a lack of, most of the
- *Use with count nouns only:* several, many, a couple of, a few, few
- *Use with noncount nouns only:* a good deal of, a great deal of, (not) much, a little, little

Be careful to distinguish between *a few/a little* and *few/little*. With the article, *a few* or *a little* means "not a lot, but enough."

Use *a few* with count nouns.

> There are **a few books** in the library on capital punishment.

Use *a little* with noncount nouns.

> There is **a little information** in the library on capital punishment.

Without the article, *few* or *little* means "not enough."

> There are **few** female **leaders** in the world. (count noun; not enough female leaders)

> My mother has **little hope** that this will change. (noncount noun; not much hope)

DESTINATIONS

For quick reference charts and practices for identifying count and noncount nouns, and the articles and quantifiers to use with them, visit the Purdue University *OWL* at <http://owl.english.purdue.edu/handouts/esl/eslcount.html>.

For lists of recommended Web resources in reading, writing, vocabulary, grammar, and other topics, organized by level, visit the *ESL Independent Study Lab* at Lewis & Clark University at <http://www.lclark.edu/~krauss/toppicks/toppicks.html>.

To explore a variety of topics to write about, as well as a well-rounded selection of other study areas, visit "Resources for English Language and Culture" at Ohio University's *Ohio ESL* at <http://www.ohiou.edu/esl/english/index.html>.

To find suggestions and strategies for investigating the English language on the Web, visit "Grammar Safari" at the LinguaCenter of the University of Illinois, Urbana-Champaign at <http://deil.lang.uiuc.edu/web.pages/grammarsafari.html#Common>. ■

---

25 | Verbs and Verb Phrases

"For me, words are a form of action, capable of influencing change." —INGRID BENGIS, writer

English verbs are complicated, and if you are a nonnative speaker, you probably still have questions about them, even after studying English for many years. This chapter addresses some of the trickier points of using verbs in English.

EXPRESS!

Learning to use English verbs correctly can be a daunting task. Equip yourself with a good grammar reference and an ESL dictionary so that when questions arise, you can find the answers. Get in the habit, too, of jotting down verb phrases that you don't understand as you are reading and listening—and then search for their meaning in your reference books or ask your English-speaking friends for clarification.

Recommended Grammar and Usage References

> Azar, Betty S. *Basic English Grammar (English as a Second Language)*. 2nd ed. New York: Prentice Hall, 1995.
> Steer, Jocelyn, and Karen Carlisi. *The Advanced Grammar Book*. 2nd ed. New York: Newbury, 1997.

Recommended ESL Dictionary

> *Longman Dictionary of American English*. 2nd ed. New York: Longman, 1997.

a Helping Verbs and Main Verbs

Helping verbs—*be, have, do,* and the modal auxiliary verbs—can be combined with main verbs to create tenses and to indicate different attitudes. Helping verbs (HV) always appear before main verbs (MV).

> HV HV MV   HV   MV
> The woman has been waiting for many hours. Do you want to wait?

When they are combined in a verb phrase, helping and main verbs always take this order:

> Modal + form of *have* + form of *be* + main verb
>
> She could   have   been   writing.
>
>   Has she   started the letter yet?

***Have, be,* and *do*.**   *Have, be,* and *do* change form to indicate tenses.

> She **is** sleeping. She **has been** sleeping for three days. She **didn't** choose to.

1. *Have, has,* or *had* + past participle. Form the perfect tenses with *have* and the past participle (*-ed* form). See pages 162–164 for a list of the past participles of irregular verbs.

   Use the present perfect to indicate that an action may continue or still has the possibility of continuing in the future.

   I have ~~live~~ *lived* here for three months.

   My mother has never ~~uses~~ *used* a computer.

   Use the past perfect to indicate one action in the past that occurs before another action in the past.

   After they had ~~talk~~ *talked* about the plan for many weeks, they decided it wouldn't work.

2. **Form of *be* + present participle.** Form the progressive tenses with a form of *be*—*am, is, are, being, been, was, were*—and the present participle (*-ing* form). Use a progressive tense to indicate ongoing actions during a time period.

   Marge is ~~drive~~ *driving* the bus to San Francisco.

   While he was ~~study~~ *studying*, the phone rang.

3. *Do, does,* or *did* + base form. *Do* is used in questions and negatives, or provides special emphasis in a sentence.

   Did they **carry** that heavy canoe for five miles?

   The weary traveler **didn't want** to cook. But she **did want** to eat.

Modals. Modal auxiliaries express an attitude about a situation. To be polite, for example, you can ask, "*Would* you open the door, please?" Choose the modal that best expresses your attitude.

   Permission (from informal to formal): *can, could, may, would you mind* (*if* + past tense)
   Ability: *can, be able to*
   Advice: *should, ought to, had better*
   Necessity: *have to, must*
   Lack of necessity: *not have to, not need to*
   Possibility (from more sure to less sure): *can, may, could, might*
   Conclusion: *must (have)*
   Expectation: *should, ought to*

Polite requests (from informal to formal): *can, will, could, would you mind* (+ *-ing*)

1. **Modal + base form of verb.**   Use the base form of a verb after a modal that expresses present or future time.

   Jacquie can ~~plays~~ ^{play} the guitar very well.

   In *have to, need to, be able to,* and *ought to,* retain the *to.*

   We **have to** write a ten-page paper.

2. **Modal +** *have* **+ past participle.**   Modals that give advice or express possibility, expectation, and conclusion have a perfect verb form. Use the perfect form to express past time.

   Where is Sue? She **should have been** here by now.

DESTINATION

For an excellent discussion and examples of English verb phrases from a linguist's point of view, visit Daniel Kies' *HyperTextBooks* at the College of DuPage at <http://papyr.com/hypertextbooks/engl_126/ph_verb.htm>. ∎

b Gerunds and Infinitives

Both gerunds (*-ing* forms) and infinitives (*to* forms) can be used as the objects of verbs. However, certain verbs in English require that you use a gerund, not an infinitive, or an infinitive, not a gerund. Other verbs take both gerunds and infinitives as objects, but sometimes the form you choose changes the meaning of the sentence.

INFINITIVE (*to* + base form of verb)

I want ^{to} go with you.

GERUND (base form of verb + *-ing*)

He enjoys ^{jogging} ~~to jog~~ in the park.

Use an infinitive after these verbs.

afford, agree, appear, arrange, ask, beg, claim, consent, decide, deserve, expect, fail, hesitate, hope, intend, learn, manage, mean, need, offer, plan, pretend, promise, refuse, seem, threaten, wait, wish

Use a gerund after these verbs.

admit, anticipate, appreciate, avoid, complete, consider, delay, deny, discuss, dislike, enjoy, finish, can't help, keep, mention, miss, postpone, practice, quit, recall, recollect, recommend, resent, resist, risk, suggest, tolerate, understand

Use either a gerund or infinitive after these verbs. Your choice will not affect the meaning of the sentence.

begin, can't bear, can't stand, continue, hate, like, prefer, start

Use a gerund or infinitive depending on your meaning.

Try **to be** nice. (make an attempt to be nice)

Try **being** nice for a change. (do an experiment; you've never been nice before)

Did you remember **to wash** the car? (didn't forget to wash the car)

Do you remember **washing** the car last month? (do you recall washing the car)

Verbs like those listed below change their meaning when followed by an infinitive or a gerund.

forget (to be): not remember
(never) forget (being): always remember
regret (to be): feel sorry about
regret (being): feel sorry about a *past* action
remember (to be): not forget
remember (being): recall, bring to mind
stop (to be): stop in order to be
stop (being): interrupt an action
try (to be): make an attempt to be
try (being): do an experiment

Use a gerund after a preposition.

Carla has been worried about **passing** her statistics course.

Mrs. Short apologized for **interrupting** our conversation.

Follow transitive verbs with a noun or pronoun + infinitive.   A transitive verb is a verb that has a direct object. This means that the verb has an effect on, or does something to, that object. The object must be stated.

> I told *her* to write me a letter.

Transitive verbs include the following.

> advise, allow, cause, challenge, convince, encourage, forbid, force, hire, instruct, invite, order, persuade, remind, require, tell, urge, warn

Use the base form of the verb after *have, let,* and *make.*   Instead of being followed by an infinitive, these verbs are followed by a noun or pronoun and the base form of the verb. Omit the *to* before the verb.

> I had my mother *to* cut my hair.

c Two- and Three-Word Verbs

Some verbs in English consist of two or three words. These verbs usually have a main verb and a preposition. These verbs are idioms—you can't understand the meaning of the verb simply by knowing the separate meaning of each of the two or three words. For example, the verb *put off* ("to postpone") has a completely different meaning from *put up with* ("to tolerate"). *Look after* means "to take care of," but *look into* means "to explore or investigate."

Two-word verbs that are transitive (take a direct object) are either separable, meaning the object can be placed before or after the preposition, or they are inseparable, meaning the verb and the preposition cannot be separated.

> **SEPARABLE**   Lee **checked** the book **out** from the library.
>
> Lee **checked out** the book from the library.

But note that if the object is a pronoun, the pronoun *must* come before the preposition.

> Gary checked out *it* from the library.

> **INSEPARABLE**   The frantic student stayed *up* all night up to study.
>
> Please look after your brother look.

Examples of Two- and Three-Word Verbs

Verb	Meaning
call off	cancel
come across*	encounter unintentionally
cut down on*	reduce the amount of
do over	repeat
figure out	solve a problem
get along with*	have harmonious relations
keep up with*	maintain the same level
make up	invent
pick out	make a selection
run into*	meet by chance
show up*	appear, arrive
stand up for*	defend, support
take after*	resemble, look alike

*Inseparable

There are many other two- and three-word verbs in English in addition to these.

26 | Proofreading in English

"I've never seen a monument erected for a pessimist." —PAUL HARVEY, broadcast journalist

Always proofread your papers carefully before you hand in the final copy. Here is a list of common proofreading problems and their solutions; add your own typical problems and then check for them each time you proofread a paper.

1. Does every clause have a subject? (Exception: commands such as "Sit down!")

   It is difficult to write in English.

2. Are any sentence elements repeated unnecessarily?

   ADJECTIVE CLAUSES   The store that I told you about ~~it~~ closed down.

SUBJECTS   My brother he~~he~~ is the director of
                        the hospital.

MULTIPLE CONNECTORS   Although the employee was dili-
                        gent, ~~but~~ she was fired.

3. Are all necessary helping verbs and main verbs included?

    The teacher ^was^ extremely helpful.

    The plane ^is^ leaving right now.

4. Do all verbs used with third-person singular nouns and
    pronouns end in *-s*?

    The library close ^s^ at 5:00 today.

5. Do all past participles end in *-ed*? (See pages 162–164 for a
    list of verbs with irregular past participles.)

    PASSIVE VOICE   The documents were alter ^ed^ by the
                            thief.
    PAST PERFECT TENSE   Juan had finish ^ed^ the race before
                            Chuck came.
    PARTICIPLE ADJECTIVES   She was frighten ^ed^ by the dark.

6. Are *-ing* endings on adjectives used for active meanings,
    and *-ed* endings for passive meanings? (See page 167 for an
    explanation of passive voice.)

    Her work is satisfying. Joan does satisfying work. (active)

    She is satisfied by her work. She is a satisfied employee. (passive)

Check These Pairs
amusing/amused by
annoying/annoyed by
boring/bored by
confusing/confused by
embarrassing/embarrassed by
exciting/excited by (or about)
frightening/frightened by
interesting/interested in
irritating/irritated by
satisfying/satisfied with

7. Are adverbs placed correctly?

Adverbs can't be placed between a verb and its object.

She answered ~~slowly~~ the question. *(slowly)*

Adverbs of frequency can't be placed before the verb *be*.

Louise ~~regularly~~ is late for class. *(regularly)*

Adverbs of frequency can't be placed after other verbs.

Harold arrives ~~often~~ late to class. *(often)*

ESL Index

You probably have other questions about English grammar or punctuation that we haven't covered in this part of *SF Express*—questions that native speakers also ask. Find your topic in this index, or check the index in the back of the book.

PART
SEVEN

Punctuation and Mechanics

27 | Commas

"A kiss can be a comma, a question mark, or an exclamation point."
                                                —MISTINGUETT, dancer

---

EXPRESS!

Every comma in a sentence should be placed for a reason: to mark a pause, to set off a unit, to keep words from running together. As signals, commas aren't as strong as semicolons, which typically appear at major intersections between clauses. And they are certainly not as forceful as periods, which mark the ends of sentences. Instead, commas make a reader slow down and pay attention to the words and ideas they set off. For this reason, it's just as important to omit commas where they aren't needed as it is to include them where they are.

---

a | Before a Coordinating Conjunction in a Compound Sentence

Coordinating conjunctions—*and, or, nor, for, but, yet,* and *so*—link independent clauses. Clauses are described as *independent* when they can stand on their own as sentences. Joining two independent clauses with a comma and a coordinating conjunction produces a compound sentence.

> West Texas can seem empty, yet the vastness of its high plains is part of its appeal.

Do not put the comma after the conjunction, a common error.

> My friends shared my opinion, but, they were afraid to say so.

Do not use a comma alone to link independent clauses. Linking independent clauses with a comma alone produces the error called a *comma splice.* Add a conjunction to indicate the relationship between the clauses.

> The plane to Atlanta was late, so we missed our connecting flight to Indianapolis.

b After an Introductory Word Group

Phrases. Commas are generally used after introductory phrases of more than three or four words.

> To appreciate the pleasures of driving in snow, you have to live in Michigan or Wisconsin.

> Over the loud objections of all the Jeep's occupants, I turned off the main road.

When an introductory phrase is short and the sentence is clear without the punctuation, you can omit the comma, although you won't be wrong to include it.

> For now I'll abstain from voting.

Use a comma to help avoid confusion or misreading, for example, after an introductory prepositional phrase or verbal.

> Stranded, the hikers headed due south.

> In Louisiana, state laws are still influenced by the Napoleonic Code.

Clauses. Always use a comma after an introductory subordinate clause. Subordinate clauses are signaled by words such as *although, if, when, because, as, after, before, since, unless,* and *while.*

> Although the vote was close, we passed the motion.

c With Nonrestrictive Modifiers

Use commas to mark nonrestrictive (nonessential) modifiers. A nonrestrictive, or nonessential, modifier is one that adds information to a sentence but can be removed without radically altering its basic meaning. Observe what happens when nonessential modifiers are removed from some sentences; some information is lost, but good sense is maintained.

Adjective phrases.

WITH COMMAS— NONRESTRICTIVE   The police officers, who looked sharp in their dress uniforms, marched in front of the mayor's car.

| LOGICAL WITHOUT MODIFIER | The police officers marched in front of the mayor's car. |

Do not use commas around restrictive, or essential, modifiers. Restrictive modifiers cannot be removed from a sentence without affecting its meaning. When an essential modifier is removed from a sentence, the sense of the sentence is lost.

| NO COMMAS— RESTRICTIVE | Diamonds that are synthetically produced are more perfect than natural diamonds. |
| NOT LOGICAL | Diamonds are more perfect than natural diamonds. |

A good general rule: Any clause introduced by *that* will be restrictive and should not be surrounded by commas.

The committee that I chair meets every Monday.

Appositives. An appositive—a noun or noun equivalent that follows a noun and gives additional information about it—can be restrictive or nonrestrictive. Use commas to enclose only nonrestrictive (nonessential) appositives.

Colleen O'Brien, our neighborhood-watch coordinator, was arrested last week for shoplifting.

Tom Robbins' novel *Half Asleep in Frog Pajamas* demonstrates Robbins' talent for using words creatively to reveal their underlying origins and metaphors.

d To Set Off Contrasts and Transitional Expressions

Use commas to mark contrasting elements and transitional expressions (including conjunctive adverbs such as *however, moreover, therefore,* and *nevertheless*).

Owning a car in most cities is a necessity, not a luxury.

Althea studied hard; therefore, she passed the examination easily.

When a contrasting clause comes after a main clause, use a comma to set it off. Also set off elements that follow a main clause when the additional thought is incidental or additional. Such clauses may be signaled by words such as *although, though, if, when, because, as, after, before, since, unless, while,* and *that is.*

We will attend the judge's lecture, which is scheduled to last an hour.

When the additional clause is closely related to the main idea
of the sentence, commas are not used. This is often a judgment
call; writers won't agree in every case.

The flag was lowered͵/while the military band played taps.

The police officers found the window broken͵/when they arrived.

e To Set Off Parenthetical Elements, Interjections, Direct Address, and Tag Questions

When these interruptions come in the middle of a sentence,
be sure to set them off with a pair of commas.

The senators͵it seems͵are eager for a filibuster.

It is interesting͵Ms. Howard͵that your story differs so much
from Ms. Liu's.

So you believe the world is flat͵do you?

f To Set Off Absolute Phrases

Absolutes are phrases made up of nouns and participles.

His head shaved͵Martin was in the Marines now.

The pioneers pressed forward across the desert͵their water almost gone.

g With Items in a Series

Use commas to link more than two items in a series. Commas keep the items in a series from colliding.

The mapmaker had omitted the capital cities of Idaho͵New
York͵and Delaware!

Use commas to link coordinate adjectives in a series. Coordinate adjectives modify the noun they precede, not each other. If
adjectives can be linked with the word *and,* they are coordinate.
Coordinates can also be switched around without major changes
in meaning.

David is a sarcastic, vindictive, and slightly frazzled secretary.

David is a vindictive, slightly frazzled, and sarcastic secretary.

In contrast, do not use commas between noncoordinate adjectives in a series. Noncoordinate adjectives work together to modify a term. They cannot be switched around or have *and* inserted between them.

> He drives a shiny, blue Mustang.

h With Quotations

> "Experience," said Oscar Wilde, "is the name everyone gives to their mistakes."

> Said P. G. Wodehouse, "I always advise people never to give advice."

i In Dates, Addresses, and Numbers

Dates. In American usage, commas separate the day from the year. A year is enclosed by commas if it appears in the middle of a sentence.

> Germany expanded World War II on June 22, 1941, when its armies invaded Russia.

Commas aren't required when only the month and year are given.

> World War II began in September, 1939.

Addresses. Commas ordinarily separate street addresses, cities, states, and countries. When these items occur in the middle of a sentence, they are enclosed by commas.

> Though born in London, England, Denise Levertov is considered an American writer.

Commas aren't used between states and zip codes.

> Austin, Texas 78712

Numbers. Commas separate units of three but are optional in four-digit numbers.

> 4,110 or 4110
>
> 1,235,470

Do not use commas in decimals, social security numbers, street addresses, telephone numbers, or zip codes.

j Unnecessary Commas

No comma separates a subject from a verb. This common error usually occurs when the full subject is more complex than usual.

> What happened to the team since last season͵isn't clear.

What happened to the team is the subject of the sentence, so it shouldn't be separated from the verb *is* with a comma.

No comma separates compound subjects, predicates, or objects.

> The Mississippi͵and the Missouri are two of the United States' great rivers.

> We toured the museum͵and then explored the monument.

> Alexander broke his promise to his agent͵and his contract with his publisher.

No comma introduces a series. If any punctuation mark is needed, it will usually be a colon, not a comma.

> States with impressive national parks include͵California, Utah, Arizona, and New Mexico.

No commas around essential modifiers. When a modifying phrase is essential, it should not be set off with commas (see 27c).

> What Asha observed͵as a civic volunteer͵changed her opinion of journalists.

---

28 | Semicolons and Colons

"*An idea is a feat of association.*"
—ROBERT FROST, poet

EXPRESS!

Using semicolons is more a matter of style than grammatical correctness. Strictly speaking, a period can almost always replace a semi-

(continued)

Express! (continued)

colon in joining two independent clauses. However, a period declares
a full stop between two sentences, while a semicolon suggests a slow-
ing down, a pause. A semicolon signals to readers that the two sentences on either side of the semicolon are closely related in thought.

a Semicolons **;**

Use semicolons when you need punctuation stronger than a
comma, but weaker than a period.

To link related independent clauses.   Often the clause
after a semicolon will clarify, add information to, or contrast with
the clause before the semicolon.

> Give Matthew the book$\overset{;}{_\wedge}$it belongs to him.

To set off conjunctive adverbs and transitions.   Independent clauses can be joined by conjunctive adverbs such as *however, therefore, nevertheless, moreover,* and *consequently,* and transitional expressions such as *indeed, in fact, at any rate, for example, as a
result,* and *on the other hand.* When they are, use a semicolon before
the expression.

> Good films often spawn sequels$\overset{;}{_\wedge}$however, the sequels rarely
> match the originals in quality.

> The film's prerelease publicity had been enormous$\overset{; \ as}{_{\wedge\wedge}}$A result,
> opening-day crowds broke all records.

Caution: Using a comma instead of a semicolon in these situations
produces a comma splice—a serious punctuation error.

**To separate items in a list that contains commas or
other punctuation.**

> Bob Hope's films include *Road to Morocco,* which also features
> Bing Crosby and Dorothy Lamour$\overset{;}{_\wedge}$ *The Paleface,* a comic
> western with Jane Russell as Calamity Jane$\overset{;}{_\wedge}$and *The Seven Lit-
> tle Foys,* a biography about vaudeville performer Eddie Foy, Sr.

Unnecessary semicolons.

**NO SEMICOLON BETWEEN A DEPENDENT AND
INDEPENDENT CLAUSE**

Although director Alfred Hitchcock once said that actors
should be treated like cattle; he won fine performances from
many of them.

**NO SEMICOLON BETWEEN AN INDEPENDENT CLAUSE
AND A PREPOSITIONAL PHRASE**

In the tradition of the finest Hollywood directors; many
young filmmakers regularly exceed their budgets.

NO SEMICOLON TO INTRODUCE A LIST

Paul Robeson performed in several distinguished films; *Show-
boat, Song of Freedom, King Solomon's Mines.*

b Colons :

Use colons to point to ideas, lists, quotations, or clauses you
wish to emphasize. A colon always follows an independent clause.

To direct readers to examples, explanations, or significant words or phrases.

Orson Welles' greatest problem may also have been his greatest achievement; the brilliance of his first film, *Citizen Kane.*

Making a film is like writing a paper; it absorbs all the time
you can give it.

To direct readers to lists after independent clauses.

Besides *Citizen Kane,* Welles directed, produced, or acted in
many movies; *The Magnificent Ambersons, Journey into Fear,*
and *Macbeth,* to name a few.

Don't use colons after expressions such as *for example, such
as, including,* or *that is.* The colon is intended to replace these expressions.

Shoestring budgets have produced many successful films such
as: *Flashdance, Breaking Away,* and *Sling Blade.*

However, colons are used after phrases that more specifically announce a list, such as *including these, as follows,* and *such as the following.*

Don't use colons after linking verbs, or between a preposition and its object.

> Among the many successful films produced on shoestring budgets are *Flashdance, Breaking Away,* and *Sling Blade.*
>
> Katharine Hepburn starred in *Little Women, The Philadelphia Story,* and *The African Queen.*

To direct readers to pay special attention to quotations or dialogue.

> We recalled Dirty Harry's memorable challenge, "Make my day!"

However, use commas with most dialogue labels or tags.

> As Dirty Harry said, "Make my day!"

To separate titles from subtitles, numbers in time expressions, and chapter and verse in biblical passages.   Colons also follow the salutation in business letters.

> "Darkest Night: Hollywood and *Film Noir*"
>
> 12:35 p.m.
>
> Matthew 3:1 (but in MLA style, Matthew 3.1)
>
> Dear Mr. Ebert:

E-Tips   "Smileys," or "emoticons," are characters created from various typographical elements. These may appear in email or other electronic environments to express feelings or opinions ranging from delight to surprise to disapproval. Emoticons should typically be reserved for informal communications.

smiley face	: -)
frowney face	: - (
wink	; -)
bored	: - |
yawn	: - o
hug	[ ]

29 Quotation Marks

"Next to the originator of a good sentence is the first quoter of it."
—RALPH WALDO EMERSON, philosopher and essayist

Quotation marks, which always occur in pairs, highlight what appears between them—namely titles, dialogue, and specific words.

EXPRESS!

Titles to be enclosed in quotation marks include the following. For a list of titles that appear in *italic* (or underlined), see page 213.

chapters of books	"Lessons from the Pros"
magazine articles	"Is the Stock Market Too High?"
journal articles	"Vai Script and Literacy"
newspaper articles	"Inflation Heats Up"
newspaper sections	"Living in Style"
TV episodes	"Caroline and the Letter"
radio episodes	"McGee Goes Crackers"
short stories	"Araby"
short poems	"The Red Wheelbarrow"
songs	"The Star-Spangled Banner"

---

a To Set Off Direct Quotations

Around short selections borrowed word for word from sources. In MLA documentation (Chapter 10), quotation marks go before the parenthetical citation. (See pages 54 and 55, especially 9c, on indicating omissions to quoted material and on introducing and framing quotations.)

> According to Kathleen Hall Jamieson, a memorable phrase can sum up a speech and become "the hook on which we hang it in memory" (90).

Note: Borrowed material that is longer than four lines (in MLA style) or more than forty words (in APA style) is not enclosed by quotation marks. Instead, these longer passages are handled as block quotations. (See page 63 for MLA; page 102 for APA.)

To mark dialogue. When writing a passage with several speakers, start a new paragraph each time the speaker changes.

> "Kitty has no discretion in her coughs," said her father; "she times them ill."
>
> "I do not cough for my own amusement," replied Kitty fretfully. —Jane Austen, *Pride and Prejudice*

With quotations introduced, interrupted, or followed by *said, remarked, observed,* or a similar expression.

> Benjamin Disraeli observed, "It is much easier to be critical than to be correct."
>
> "If the world were a logical place," Rita Mae Brown notes, "men would ride sidesaddle."

In quotations within quotations. Use double quotation marks (" ") around most quoted material; use single quotation marks (' ') to mark quotations within quotations.

> Jane said, "I love folk songs from the 1960s."
>
> Jane said, "My favorite is 'If I Had a Hammer.'"

b To Cite the Titles of Short Works

These include titles of songs, essays, magazine and newspaper articles, TV episodes, unpublished speeches, chapters of books, and short poems (see Express! page 207). Titles of longer works appear in *italic* (see Express! page 213).

> "Love Is Just a Four-Letter Word" [song]

c With Other Punctuation Marks

After commas and periods.   Place commas and periods inside closing quotation marks, except when you are using MLA documentation (see page 63).

> "There is no such thing as a moral book or an immoral book," says Oscar Wilde. "Books are well-written or badly written. That is all."

MLA STYLE

> Mike Rose argues that we hurt education if we think of it "in limited or limiting ways" (3).

Before colons and semicolons.   Place colons and semicolons outside closing quotation marks.

> Riley claimed to be "a human calculator": he did quadratic equations in his head.

> The young Cassius Clay bragged about being "the greatest"; his opponents in the ring soon learned he wasn't boasting.

With question marks, exclamation points, and dashes.   These punctuation marks can fall either inside or outside the closing quotation marks. They fall inside when they apply only to the quotation.

> When Mrs. Rattle saw her hotel room, she muttered, "Good grief!"

> She turned to her husband and said, "Do you really expect me to stay here?"

They fall outside the closing quotation mark when they apply to the complete sentence.

> Who was it that said, "Truth is always the strongest argument"?

Other quotations.   No extra punctuation is required when a quotation runs smoothly into a sentence you have written.

> Abraham Lincoln observed that "in giving freedom to the slave we assure freedom to the free."

d To Draw Attention to Specific Words or Expressions

People clearly mean different things when they write about "democracy."

Use quotation marks to show when you are using words or expressions ironically, sarcastically, or derisively. But don't overdo the use of quotation marks for adding emphasis; doing so makes your text harder to read.

The clerk at the desk directed the tourists to their "suites"— bare rooms crowded with cots. A bathroom down the hall would serve as the "spa."

30   Apostrophes

"The creative impulses of man are always at war with the possessive impulses."
—VAN WYCK BROOKS, literary critic and cultural historian

EXPRESS!

Probably the most common apostrophe errors occur with *its/it's* and *whose/who's*. Most writers form the contractions—*it's* and *who's*—correctly. The mistakes come with the possessive forms—*its* and *whose*—because these forms deviate from the general rule of adding an apostrophe and *-s* to a singular noun.

ITS = POSSESSIVE

The dog injured its leg.

The cat licked its whiskers.

IT'S = CONTRACTION

It's time to go. (It is time to go.)

WHOSE = POSSESSIVE

Whose watch is this?

Whose house is this?

WHO'S = CONTRACTION

Who's going to the movie? (Who is going to the movie?)

a To Form Possessive Nouns

Add an apostrophe + -s to most singular nouns and to plural nouns that do not end in -s.

> a dog's life
>
> geese's behavior
>
> the NCAA's ruling
>
> children's imaginations

Form the possessive of singular nouns ending in -s or -z with either an apostrophe + -s or just the apostrophe. Use one form or the other consistently.

> the countess's jewels *or* the countess' jewels
>
> Katz's menu or Katz' menu

Add an apostrophe (but not an -s) to plural nouns that end in -s.

> the hostesses' job
>
> the senators' parking spaces

Do not use apostrophes to make personal pronouns possessive. Personal pronouns include *my, your, her, his, our, their,* and *its.* Don't confuse the possessive pronouns *its* and *whose* with the contractions *it's* and *who's.*

> **It's** an idea that has **its** opponents up in arms.
>
> **Who's** to say **whose** opinion is right?

Use apostrophes to show possession in compound or hyphenated words. Add the apostrophe to the last word in the compound item.

> the president-elect's decision
>
> both fathers-in-law's Cadillacs

b In Contractions and Omissions

Use apostrophes in contractions to show where letters have been omitted. Such apostrophes are not optional.

> can't—cannot
>
> it's—it is or it has

you're—you are

who's—who is or who has

c In Some Plurals

The apostrophe is optional to form the plurals of numbers, symbols, individual letters, abbreviations, dates, and words used as words. Use an apostrophe when needed for the sake of clarity, but avoid an apostrophe when the -*'s* might be mistaken for a possessive.

2's and 3's or 2s and 3s	the 1990's or the 1990s
A's and B's or As and Bs	and's or *and*s
B.A.'s or B.A.s	the three CEO's or the three CEOs
two CD's or two CDs	The ACT's or the ACTs

Do not use apostrophes to form the plurals of nouns.

The company can put up signs in the neighborhood.

Do not use apostrophes to form the plurals of family names.   Form such plurals by adding an -*s* or -*es*. Form possessives by adding an apostrophe.

Singular	**Plural**	**Possessive**
Richard Clarke	the Clarkes	the Clarkes' dog
Jean James	the Jameses	the Jameses' house

d To Show Joint Ownership

When two nouns share ownership, only the second noun needs an apostrophe.

Peg and John's research grant

Vorhees and Goetz' project

When ownership is separate, each noun shows possession.   In such cases, the objects possessed are usually plural.

Peg's and John's educations

Vorhees' and Goetz' offices

31 | Other Punctuation Marks

"I personally think we developed language because of our deep need to complain."

—LILY TOMLIN, comic, actress

Titles that appear in *italic* (or underlined) include the following. For a list of titles that are enclosed in quotation marks, see page 207.

books	*All the Pretty Horses*
magazines	*Slate*
journals	*Written Communication*
newspapers	*New York Times*
films	*Casablanca*
TV shows	*Politically Incorrect*
radio shows	*All Things Considered*
plays	*Measure for Measure*
long poems	*Paradise Lost*
long musical pieces	*The Mikado*
albums	Beck's *Odelay*
paintings	Schnabel's *Adieu*
sculptures	Christo's *Running Fence*
dances	Antonio's *Goya*
ships	U.S.S. *Saratoga*
trains	the *Orient Express*
aircraft	*Enola Gay*
spacecraft	*Apollo 11*
software programs	*Microsoft Word*

a Periods

Use periods to mark the end of sentences and abbreviations.

To end statements and most commands.

Hannibal, general of Carthage, has been hailed as a genius of military strategy.

Just look at the dog.

To end indirect questions.   Indirect questions are statements that seem to have questions within them. They usually contain the words *whether* or *if,* or an interrogative pronoun such as *which* or *who.*

> Varro wondered whether Hannibal's strategy would succeed.
>
> Martha wants to know which window keeps getting stuck.

To punctuate most abbreviations.   Most abbreviations for one- or two-word expressions require periods, but state abbreviations do not.

anon.	Ms.	Dr.	Ph.D.
U.S.	WI	CA	TX

Longer abbreviations written in capital letters often don't require periods.

FBI	CIA	UNICEF	NAFTA
NOW	MADD	NATO	

To indicate decimals.

0.01	$189.99	75.47

E-Tips   Addresses for World Wide Web sites include a number of conventional marks, such as periods (called "dots"), colons, and slashes. Email addresses typically include the symbol for *at*: @.

WORLD WIDE WEB ADDRESS

http://www.uwyo.edu/

EMAIL ADDRESS

feedback@sss.whitehouse.gov

In MLA documentation, electronic addresses are enclosed in angle brackets to prevent surrounding punctuation from being mistakenly attached to the item.

<http://www.utexas.edu/>

b Question Marks

Use question marks to terminate questions or to suggest doubt.

After direct questions.

> Who fought in the Battle of Cannae?

To indicate uncertainty about dates, numbers, or statements.

> Hannibal (247?–183 B.C.) was a military tactician.

> She survived that terrible crash?

To end sentences that begin as statements but end with direct questions.

> The strategy looked fine, but would it work on the battlefield?

Don't confuse this construction with an indirect question, discussed in 31a.

With quotation marks. Place question marks outside quotation marks except when they are part of the quoted material itself.

> Was it Terence who wrote "Fortune helps the brave"?

> "Have you read any Cicero?" the teacher asked.

c Exclamation Points

Although rare in academic and business writing, exclamation points give emphasis to statements. Use only one exclamation point in a sentence.

> Don't overdo it!!!!

To express strong feelings or commands.

> Oh, no! We're lost again.   Come here now!

Don't use commas after exclamations that fall in the middle of sentences.

> "Please check your records again!" the caller demanded.

d Dashes

Use dashes to separate and call attention to ideas in sentences.

To insert a comment or call attention to information in a sentence. Dashes in the middle of a sentence are always paired.

Marie's writing style—complex, subtle, yet also incisive—earned the admiration of her colleagues.

To emphasize illustrations, examples, or summaries, or to call attention to a shift or contrast in content or tone.

Beethoven's Ninth Symphony was a great accomplishment for an artist in bad health—and completely deaf.

I'm heartened that Beck, Lou, and others are apparently able to look at the positive side of the experience—and envious.
—Jon Krakauer, *Into Thin Air*

Don't use a hyphen when a dash is required. Use hyphens to connect items; use dashes to separate items. On most computer keyboards, you can type a dash with a key combination. Or, you can type a dash using two unspaced hyphens [--]. Do not leave spaces before or after a dash.

Beethoven's music—unlike that of Mozart—uses emphatic rhythms.

Don't use too many dashes in a sentence or passage. Certainly use no more than one pair of dashes per sentence.

Mozart—recognized as a genius while still a child—produced more than 600 compositions during his life—including symphonies, operas, and concertos.

e Hyphens

Use hyphens either to put words together or to divide them between syllables.

To link some compound nouns and verbs. The conventions for hyphenating words are complicated and inconsistent. Below are some expressions that take hyphens and some that don't. When in doubt, check a dictionary or style manual.

| best-seller | mother-in-law | right-hander | cab owner |
| best man | life span | cabdriver | |

To indicate double titles, elements, functions, or attributes.

city-state   space-time   AFL-CIO

To link unit modifiers before a noun.

A *unit modifier* is a two-word modifier in which the first word modifies the second. The resulting unit modifies a following noun.

an English-speaking city   a hard-hitting exposé

When a comma between the modifying words produces nonsense, you probably have a unit modifier that requires a hyphen.

an English, speaking city (?)

But don't use hyphens to link compound modifiers following a noun.

The candidate was hardly awe-inspiring.

Don't use hyphens with *very* or with adverbs that end in *-ly*.

a very-hot day   a sharply-honed knife

In numbers from twenty-one to ninety-nine, and in fractions.

two hundred forty-six   one forty-seventh of a mile

To link prefixes to proper nouns and their corresponding adjectives.

pre-Columbian   anti-American

mid-Victorian   neo-Darwinism

In all words beginning with the prefixes *all-*, *self-*, and *ex-* or ending with the suffix *-elect*.

all-encompassing   ex-hockey player

self-contained   mayor-elect

Hyphenate most words beginning with *well-*, *ill-*, and *heavy-*.

well-dressed   ill-suited   heavy-handed

Most common nouns beginning with *un-*, *non-*, *anti-*, *pro-*, *co-*, and *pre-* are not hyphenated.

uncertainty   antislavery

coordination   prodemocracy

E-Tips

> To avoid hyphenating words or numbers at the ends of lines, turn on the word wrap function of your word processor. The word wrap will automatically eliminate end-of-line divisions. When you must divide a word, break it only at a syllable and then check a dictionary for the syllable break.

f Ellipses

Use an ellipsis (. . .) to mark a gap in a sentence or passage. Type an ellipsis using three periods or dots with spaces between them.

Where material has been omitted from direct quotations.   This material may be a word, a phrase, a sentence, or more. See 9c for MLA guidelines for using ellipses in quotations.

> To be honest . . . is to be one man picked out of ten thousand.
> —*Hamlet* 2.2

To indicate pauses or to suggest that an action is incomplete or continuing.

> The rocket rumbled on its launch pad as the countdown proceeded: "Four, three, two, . . ."

To indicate that a speaker is hesitating or that a speech has trailed off.

> "If you insist . . . ," the clerk muttered.

Spacing and punctuation.   Use correct spacing and punctuation before and after ellipsis marks. When an ellipsis mark appears in the middle of a sentence, leave a space before the first period and after the last period.

> chords of memory . . . will yet swell

If a punctuation mark occurs immediately before the ellipsis, include the mark when it makes your sentence easier to read. Then, add a space and the ellipsis.

> We are not enemies, . . . must not be enemies.

When an ellipsis occurs at the end of a complete sentence or when you delete a full sentence or more, place a period at the end of the sentence, followed by a space and then the ellipsis.

We must not be enemies. . . . The mystic chords

Use an ellipsis at the beginning of a quotation only when an incomplete sentence might be mistaken for a full one because the quoted passage opens with a capital letter.

As Falstaff puts it, ". . . God help the wicked!"

g Parentheses

Enclose extra information, a comment, or an aside in parentheses. Parentheses are less emphatic than dashes and more common than brackets.

To separate material—a word, phrase, list, or complete sentence—from the main body of a sentence or paragraph.

The flight to Colorado was quick (ninety minutes) and uneventful.

To highlight numbers or letters used to list items within the text.

The labor negotiators realized they could (1) concede on all issues immediately, (2) stonewall until the public demanded a settlement, or (3) hammer out a compromise.

With end punctuation.
Place parentheses properly either inside or outside end punctuation. When a complete sentence standing alone is surrounded by parentheses, its end punctuation belongs *inside* the end parenthesis.

The neighborhood was run-down and littered. (Some houses hadn't been painted in decades.)

When a sentence concludes with parentheses, the end punctuation for the complete sentence falls *outside* the final parentheses mark.

On the corner was a small church (actually, a converted store).

To provide source information in MLA and APA documentation.
For guidelines and examples, see 10a (MLA) and 11a (APA).

To set off acronyms.
For the first mention of an agency or organization, use the full name and indicate the appropriate

acronym in parentheses. Then you can use the acronym in the rest of your paper.

> As law has become a popular professional choice, college graduates flock in increasing numbers to testing sites for the Law School Admissions Test (LSAT). The LSAT measures logical and analytical reasoning, reading comprehension, and writing.
> —Myra and David Sadker, *Failing at Fairness:*
> *How Our Schools Cheat Girls*

h Brackets

Use brackets for special situations.

To insert comments or explanations into direct quotations.
You cannot change the words in a direct quotation, but you can add information in brackets.

> "He [George Lucas] reminded me a little of Walt Disney's version of a mad scientist."   —Steven Spielberg

Any change to an original text, even if only from an uppercase to a lowercase letter or vice versa, should be signaled with brackets.

> In *The Dinosaur Heresies,* Bakker rejects "[o]rthodox theory." Dinosaurs, he argues, are not just big reptiles with a "metabolism [that is] pitifully low compared to mammals'."

To avoid one set of parentheses falling within another.
Turn the inner pair into brackets.

> The paper included a full text of the resolution (expressing the sense of the House of Representatives on the calculation of the Consumer Price Index [H.RES.99]).

To acknowledge or highlight errors that originate in quoted material.
Enclose the word *sic* in brackets immediately after the error.

> The sign said, "We except [*sic*] no checks."

i Italics (Underlining)

Use italics or underlining to draw attention to a title, a word, or a phrase.

To set off some titles. In general, italicize titles of works that are published as independent units, such as books, magazines, journals, newspapers, films, TV shows, plays, long poems, paintings, sculptures, and software programs (see Express! page 213). Titles of shorter works appear in quotation marks (see Express! page 207). Also italicize the names of ships, trains, aircraft, and spacecraft.

Do not use italics or quotation marks with titles of major religious texts, books of the bible, or classic legal documents.

> the Bible   Genesis
>
> the Qur'an   the Declaration of Independence

> **E-Tips**
>
> When email will not permit underlining or italics, writers use an *underscore* (shift + hyphen) before and after a book title or other expression that would normally be italicized. Other punctuation follows the underscore.
>
> Everyone in the newsgroup might enjoy reading a review of _Trainspotting_ that appeared in this week's _New York Times_.

To set off foreign words and phrases. Latin names for biological categories such as genus and species are also italicized.

> Environmental problems haunt the *maquiladora* corridor along the U.S.–Mexican border.
>
> Mary and Louis Leakey pioneered the search for the ancestors of *Homo sapiens.*

To set off words, letters, numbers, and phrases referred to as themselves, not as what they stand for. You can use quotation marks instead, if you prefer.

> Does that word begin with an *f* or a *ph*?
>
> The word *weird* is often misspelled.

To emphasize a letter, word, or phrase.

> "That may be how *you* play volleyball," she replied.

j | Slashes

Slashes are used for a few specific functions.

To divide lines of poetry quoted within sentences.
Leave a space on either side of the slash.

> Only then does Lear understand that he has been a failure as a king: "O, I have taken / Too little care of this!"

If you quote more than three lines of verse, set the passage as a block quotation and break the lines as they appear in the poem itself. Do not use slashes.

To separate expressions that indicate a choice. Leave no space before or after the slash.

> yes/no   pass/fail

---

32 | Capital Letters, Abbreviations, and Numbers

"In order to make an apple pie from scratch, you must first create the universe."

—CARL SAGAN, astronomer

EXPRESS!

To capitalize a title, follow these three steps.

- Capitalize the first word.
- Capitalize the last word.
- Capitalize all other words *except*

  Articles (*a, an, the*)
  The *to* in infinitives (*to* grow)
  Prepositions (*in, at, on,* and so forth)
  Coordinating conjunctions (*and, but, or, for, yet, so*)

a Capital Letters

Capitalize the first word of a sentence.

It was a dark and stormy night.

Capitalize the first word of a direct quotation when it is a full sentence.   Use lowercase for quotations that continue after an interruption.

Ira asked, "Where's the Air and Space museum?"

"It's on the Mall," the guide replied, "not far from the Hirschhorn Gallery."

Don't capitalize the first word after a colon unless you want to emphasize it or unless it is part of a title.

NO CAPITAL	They ignored one detail while parking the car: a no-parking sign.
ADDED EMPHASIS	The words haunted her: Your license has expired!
PART OF TITLE	*Marilyn: The Untold Story*

Capitalize the major words in the titles of books, papers, articles, poems, and so on.

All the Trouble in the World

"Stopping by Woods on a Snowy Evening"

Capitalize the first word in lines of quoted poetry unless the poet has used lowercase letters.

Sumer is ycomen in,

Loude sing cuckoo!

—"The Cuckoo Song"

anyone lived in a pretty how town,

(with up so floating many bells down)

—E. E. Cummings, "anyone lived in a pretty how town"

Capitalize the names and titles of people. People's names are *proper nouns,* which refer to specific people, places, or things, while nouns that refer to people, places, and things in general are called *common nouns.*

Proper Nouns	Common Nouns
Emily Dickinson	poet
John	brother
Ted Kennedy	senator

Also capitalize titles associated with people.

> Justice Ruth Ginsberg   Rosa Eberly, Ph.D.
>
> R. Donald King, Dean of Liberal Arts

It is generally acceptable to capitalize a title that is being used in place of a name.

> the President or the president
>
> the Secretary of State or the secretary of state

Capitalize titles of family members if the titles are standing in place of names. Compare the two examples.

> Every night, Mother expected us to read ten pages from Jane Austen or Charles Dickens before watching television.
>
> My mother insisted that we read good literature.

Capitalize *God* when you are referring specifically to the god of the Judeo-Christian tradition, but not when you are referring to *gods* in general.

> In the Old Testament, God punished those who chose to worship the pagan gods.

Capitalize the names of national, political, or ethnic groups.

> Kenyans
>
> Australians
>
> African Americans

Capitalize the names of institutions and specific objects.

businesses	DaimlerChrysler
organizations	National Rifle Association
unions	Teamsters

schools	University of Memphis
religious figures	the Blessed Virgin
religions	Buddhism
sacred books	the Bible, the Torah
place names	Asia, France
geographic features	the Gulf of Mexico
buildings	the Empire State Building
structures	Jacob's Field
monuments	the Alamo
ships and planes	S.S. *Titanic,* Boeing 767
automobiles	Mercedes ML320
documents	the Constitution
cultural movements	Romanticism, Vorticism
historical periods	Pax Romana, Victorian Age
days and months	Wednesday, June
holidays	Halloween, Fourth of July
course titles	History 101
paintings and sculptures	*Guernica,* the *Venus de Milo*
brand names	Kleenex, Coke

Capitalize words like *river, park, street,* and *road* only when they refer to a specific road, river, or street.

| Georgetown Road | a gravel road |
| the Mississippi River | an American river |

Do not capitalize seasons or compass directions unless they are being used as a place name.

winter, spring

north, south

North America, the South

Capitalize adjectives formed from proper names.

Palestinian history   Martian expedition

Capitalize abstractions to give them special emphasis. Compare the two examples.

What is this thing called Love?

Adil had fallen in love again.

Capitalize all letters in most acronyms.

OPEC   NATO treaty

b Abbreviations

Be consistent in punctuating abbreviations and acronyms.

- Abbreviations of single words usually take periods: vols., Jan., Mr.
- Abbreviations spoken letter by letter are usually written without periods: HBO, IRS, CNN.
- Acronyms spoken as complete words do not require periods: CARE, NATO, NOW.
- Periods are usually omitted after abbreviations in technical writing unless an item might be misread without the period: *ft* for *foot, km* for *kilometer.*

Be consistent in capitalizing abbreviations and acronyms.   Capitalize the following.

- Abbreviations of words that are capitalized when written out: General Motors—GM; 98°Fahrenheit—98°F. But do not capitalize abbreviations of words not capitalized when written out: pound—lb; minutes—min.
- Most acronyms: IRS, CRT, NVC.
- B.C. and A.D. or B.C.E. and C.E.

Ordinarily, *a.m.* and *p.m.* appear in lowercase, although uppercase is acceptable.

Use the appropriate abbreviations for titles, academic degrees, and names.   Some titles are almost always abbreviated (Mr., Ms., Mrs., Jr.). Others are normally written out, although these may be abbreviated when they precede a first name or initial.

Professor Campbell	Prof. Kermit Campbell
Reverend Eagle	Rev. Ann Eagle

Use appropriate common abbreviations.   The following are appropriate in all types of writing.

businesses	IBM, A&P, MTV
organizations	NCAA, GOP
time	43 B.C.E., A.D. 1999

| temperature | 13°C, 98°F |
| places | Washington, D.C. |

The following abbreviations are appropriate in special situations, such as technical reports, footnotes, recipes, forms, and addresses. In most writing, however, the terms should be written out in full.

months	Jan., Aug.
days	Mon., Fri.
time	60 mins., 3 hrs.
weights	30 lb, 29 kg
measures	3 tsp, 26 km
book terms	p., vol., ch.
states (postal)	CA, NY, TX, WI

Some abbreviations should be used only with numerals.

Sales were 100 percent on target.

or

Sales were 100% on target.

Abbreviate common Latin terms such as *et cetera* (etc.) and *et alia* (et al.). Although these terms often appear in footnotes, use them sparingly in most formal writing. Check stylebooks to see which abbreviations are preferred in a given field.

c Numbers

Write out numbers from one to nine; use numerals for numbers larger than nine. Note, however, that MLA style recommends spelling out any number that can be expressed in one or two words.

thirteen   twenty-one   three hundred

Combine words and figures for large round numbers.

100 billion   432 million

Use numerals appropriately.

addresses	1900 East Blvd.
dates	July 4, 1776
exact amounts of money	$3.43
measurements	2.5 miles, 33°C
page and chapter numbers	page 43, Chapter 6

percentages	75 percent
scores	a 6–2 victory
statistics	average test score 530, median income $33,000
time	10:00 a.m., 2:15 p.m. (but ten in the morning, six o'clock)

Don't begin sentences with numerals. Either spell out the number or rephrase the sentence so that the numeral is not the first word.

<del>32</del> *Thirty-two* people were standing in line.

When two separate numbers occur together, write one out and use a numeral for the other.

The country acquired <del>3</del> *three* 100-million-dollar loans.

Spell out ordinal numbers: first, second, third, fourth, and so on. Don't make these words adverbs by adding *-ly*.

The <del>1st</del> *first* thing we had to do was bait our hooks.

Second<del>ly,</del> we had to learn how to cast.

33 Spelling, Dictionary, Thesaurus

"My spelling is Wobbly. It's good spelling but it Wobbles, and the letters get in the wrong places."
—A. A. MILNE, humorist and children's author

EXPRESS!

Readers react very strongly to spelling errors, so carefully edit the final draft of any paper you write. Most spelling errors involve simple words rather than difficult ones, and the toughest errors to catch are habitual ones, such as mistaking *their* for *there* and *to* for *too*.

To track your spelling trouble spots, keep a file—on disk or on paper—of the words you frequently misspell. Check your final draft against your list before you print out the final copy of your paper.

a Spelling

Proofread carefully to eliminate obvious errors.   Here are three effective proofreading techniques.

> Read a draft slowly, aloud.
> Read a draft with a pencil in hand; touch each word as you read.
> Read a draft backward to isolate individual words.

Be especially careful of words that contain the following elements.

- Words that contain *ei* or *ie*: receive, believe, foreign, counterfeit
- Words with silent letters: pneumonia, debt, answer
- Words that end in suffixes

  -able or *-ible:* laughable, visible
  -ance or *-ence*: guidance, obedience
  -ant or *-ent*: attendant, different
  -cede, -ceed, or *-sede:* precede, proceed, supersede

- Words that contain double consonants: occurrence, embarrass, exaggerate, accumulate, accommodate, recommend
- Contractions: who's, it's, you're, don't, won't, can't (see pages 211–212)
- Possessive forms: Jones's, Boz's (see page 211)
- Hyphenated words: double-edged, mothers-in-law (see pages 216–217)

Eliminate errors that result from problems with pronunciation or misreading.   You may not recognize some spelling errors until a reader points them out. The following list gives some examples of words to look for.

Incorrect	Correct
alot	a lot
alright	all right
arguement	argument
athelete	athlete
beleive	believe
definately	definitely
enviroment	environment
Febuary	February

(continued)

Incorrect	Correct
goverment	government
hankerchief	handkerchief
knowlege	knowledge
mispell	misspell
neccesary	necessary
noticable	noticeable
occured	occurred
perscription	prescription
privlege	privilege
recieve	receive
roomate	roommate
seperate	separate
supposadly	supposedly
suprise	surprise
surpress	suppress
temperture	temperature
truely	truly

When in doubt, look up the spellings of words. As you write, mark doubtful spellings and consult a dictionary after you've drafted a section of your paper. Avoid spellings labeled chiefly British, archaic, or obsolete unless you have a special reason for using them, such as a direct quotation.

Apply spelling rules—if helpful. Spelling rules in English tend to be complicated, hard to remember, and unreliable. Guidelines such as those below can help, but they never cover every exception.

- Choosing between *ei* and *ie*. In general, *i* comes before *e* except after *c*—unless *ei* has a long "*a*" sound.

believe	eight
receive	weigh

  Significant exceptions weaken even this familiar guideline.
counterfeit	either
weird	foreign

- Adding prefixes. Prefixes do not change the spelling of the stem word.

Incorrect	Correct
mispelled	misspelled
unecessary	unnecessary
dissappear	disappear

- Doubling consonants in suffixes. Generally, double consonants when adding suffixes to a one-syllable word that ends in one vowel plus a consonant.

hit	hitting
swim	swimming

Double consonants if the word ends in a vowel and a consonant and the final syllable before the suffix is stressed once the suffix has been added.

occur	occurred	occurrence
refer	referred	
begin	beginning	
control	controlling	

Don't double consonants if some other syllable is stressed once the suffix has been added.

refer	reference
accustom	accustomed

Don't double consonants if the syllable before the suffix contains more than one vowel or ends in more than one consonant.

speed	speeding
bank	banking

Dropping final *e*'s before suffixes. Drop a final silent *e* if the suffix begins with a vowel.

slide	sliding
arrange	arranging
refute	refutable

Do not drop the final *e* if the main word ends in *c* or *g* and the suffix begins with *a*; doing so causes the preceding *c*'s and *g*'s to have a hard sound, as in *cook* and *gun*.

Incorrect	Correct
replacable	replaceable
changable	changeable

Do not drop a final silent *e* if the suffix begins with a consonant.

bereave	bereavement
hate	hateful

- Adding suffixes to words ending in *y.* Change *y* to *i* after a consonant.

| merry | merriment |
| fancy | fanciful |

Do not change *y* to *i* in one-syllable words.

| pry | prying |
| play | playing |

Do not change *y* to *i* after a vowel or in proper names.

| employ | employing |
| Alice Petry | the Petrys |

- Pay close attention to homonyms—words that sound or look alike. These words cause many errors because they are easily confused. As with other difficult words, build a list of your habitual troublemakers. Below is a list of some common troublemakers.

Homonyms

all ready (set to go)	already (by now)	
altar (table)	alter (change)	
bare (empty, clear)	bear (carry)	
board (group/plank/ climb on)	bored (uninterested)	
brake (stop)	break (fracture)	
capital (seat of government)	capitol (government building)	
cite (point out)	sight (see)	site (location)
complement (make complete)	compliment (praise)	
council (group)	counsel (advice/lawyer)	
desert (abandon/ arid place)	dessert (treat)	
gorilla (large ape)	guerrilla (soldier)	
hear (perceive sound)	here (this place)	
its (possessive)	it's (contraction for *it is*)	
lead (to direct/metal)	led (past tense of *to lead*)	
lessen (decrease)	lesson (instruction)	
passed (went by/ met standards)	past (what's occurred)	
patience (tolerance)	patients (people under medical care)	

peace (harmony)	piece (part or portion)	
principal (head of school/most important)	principle (standard/ moral guide)	
road (highway)	rode (past tense of *ride*)	
stationary (not moving)	stationery (writing material)	
their (possessive)	there (in that place)	they're (contraction for *they are*)
threw (past tense of *throw*)	through (across)	
throne (royal seat)	thrown (past participle of *throw*)	
weak (not strong)	week (seven days)	
wear (to have on)	where (place)	
weather (climate)	whether (if/choice)	
whose (possessive)	who's (contraction for *who is*)	
your (possessive)	you're (contraction for *you are*)	

- Spell plurals correctly. Add -*s* to most nouns to form the plural.

toy	toys
picture	pictures
demonstration	demonstrations

Add -*es* when the plural adds a syllable to the pronunciation of a noun. This occurs most often with words ending in -*s*, -*sh*, -*ch*, -*z*, or -*x*.

dish	dishes
summons	summonses
arch	arches
hex	hexes

Learning some general guidelines will help you spot troublesome cases.

- Recognize common irregular plurals, such as *man/men; woman/women;* and *mouse/mice.*
- Learn common plural patterns.

Consonant + -*y* = -*ies*
| family | families |
| party | parties |

Consonant + -o = -oes

| hero | heroes |
| tomato | tomatoes |

Vowel + -o =   *-os*

| video | videos |
| patio | patios |

-f =   *-ves*

| thief | thieves |
| scarf | scarves |

• Check the plural of compound words, especially if they are hyphenated expressions. Usually the first word in the compound is pluralized.

attorney general	attorneys general
father-in-law	fathers-in-law
passerby	passersby

E-Tips

A spelling checker on a word processor will find misspelled words—as long as the mistakes aren't legitimate words on their own. For example, a spelling checker will signal if you spell *supposed* as "suposed" but not if you've omitted the *d* at the end of the word, because *suppose* is a correctly spelled word by itself.

After you've run the spelling checker, proofread the draft again to find errors computers don't catch, such as homonyms and usage errors.

---

b Dictionary and Thesaurus

Own a desk-sized dictionary.   Desk or collegiate dictionaries typically contain enough entries for most routine writing jobs.

Consult an unabridged dictionary when necessary.
When you are looking for a rare, obscure, or old word, or when you need comprehensive or historical information about a term, consult an unabridged dictionary, routinely available in the library reference room. The *Oxford English Dictionary* is the most famous unabridged dictionary.

Use a pocket dictionary as a convenience.   Rely on a pocket dictionary for correct spellings and basic meanings. It will contain fewer entries, shorter definitions, and sketchier etymologies (word origins) than do college dictionaries.

Use a thesaurus judiciously.   A *thesaurus* is a dictionary of synonyms (and usually antonyms) to help you find the best word for a particular situation. Be sure that any synonyms you select match both denotatively and connotatively the words you intend to replace.

Glossary of Grammatical Terms

absolute.   A phrase that modifies an entire sentence. Absolutes are often infinitive or participial phrases. Unlike other modifying phrases, absolutes do not necessarily modify a word or phrase standing near them.

> **To put it politely,** Connie is irritating.
>
> She will publish the entire story, **space permitting.**
>
> **Scripts discarded, props disassembled, costumes locked away in trunks,** the annual Shakespeare festival concluded.

adjective.   A word that modifies a noun or pronoun. Some adjectives describe the words they modify, explaining how many, which color, which one, and so on.

> an **unsuccessful** coach   a **green** motel
>
> the **lucky** one   a **sacred** icon

Such adjectives frequently have comparative and superlative forms.

> the **blacker** cat   the **happiest** people

Other adjectives limit or specify the words they modify.

> **this** adventure   **every** penny
>
> **each** participant   **neither** video

Proper nouns can also serve as adjectives.

> **Texan** wildlife   **Eisenhower** era

adverb.   A word that modifies a verb, an adjective, or another verb. Adverbs explain where, when, and how.

>   adverb   verb
>
> Bud **immediately** *suspected* foul play at the Hutton mansion.

>   adverb   adjective
>
> It seemed **extremely** *odd* to him that Mrs. Hutton should load a large burlap sack into the trunk of her Mercedes.

>   adverb   adverb
>
> Mrs. Hutton replied **rather** *evasively* when Bud questioned her about what she was up to.

Some adverbs modify complete sentences.

> adverb
>
> **Obviously,** Mr. Hutton had been murdered!

appositive.   A word or phrase that stands next to a noun and modifies it by restating or expanding its meaning. Note that appositives are ordinarily surrounded by commas. (See 27c.)

> Connie Lim, **editor of the paper and an arch-liberal,** was furious when former President Clinton gave his only campus interview to Sue Wesley, **chair of the Young Republicans.**

articles.   The words, **the, a,** and **an** used before a noun. **The** is called a **definite article** because it points to something specific: **the** book, **the** church, **the** criminal. **A** and **an** are indefinite articles because they refer more generally: **a** book, **a** church, **a** criminal. (See 24b.)

auxiliary verbs.   Verbs, usually some form of *be, do,* or *have,* that combine with other verbs to show various relations of tense, voice, mood, and so on. All the words in boldface are auxiliary verbs: **has** seen, **will be** talking, **would have been** going, **are** investigating, **did** mention, **should** prefer. Auxiliary verbs are also known as helping verbs. (See 25a.)

conjunctions, coordinating.   The words *and, or, nor, for, but, yet,* and *so* used to link words, phrases, and clauses that serve equivalent functions in a sentence. A coordinating conjunction is used to join two independent clauses or two dependent clauses.

> Oscar **and** Marie directed the play.

> Oscar liked the story, **but** Marie did not.

conjunctions, subordinating.   Words or expressions such as *although, because, if, since, before, after, when, even though, in order that,* and *while* that relate subordinate or dependent clauses to independent ones (see 27c). Subordinating conjunctions introduce subordinate clauses.

> subordinate clause
>
> **When** the show opened, audiences stayed away.

gender.   A classification of nouns and pronouns as masculine (*actor, muscleman, he*), feminine (*actress, midwife, she*), or neuter (*tree, it*).

gerund.   A verb form used as a noun: *smiling, biking, walking.* (See 25b.) Most gerunds end in -**ing** and, consequently, look identical to the present participle.

> **GERUND**   **Smiling** is good for the health.

> **PARTICIPLE**   A **smiling** critic is dangerous.

However, gerunds function as nouns, while participles act as modifiers. Gerunds usually appear in the present tense, but they can take other forms.

> **Having been criticized** made Brian angry.
>
> gerund in past tense, passive voice, acting as subject of the sentence

> **Being asked** to play an encore was a compliment Otto enjoyed.
>
> gerund in present tense, passive voice, as subject of sentence

infinitive.   A verbal that can usually be identified by the word **to** preceding the base form of a verb: *to strive, to seek, to find, to endure.* Infinitives do take other forms to show various tenses and voices: *to be seeking, to have found, to have been found.* Infinitives can act as nouns, adjectives, adverbs, and absolutes (see 25b).

	subject
INFINITIVE AS NOUN	**To capture** a market is not easy.

	modifies the noun *posters*
INFINITIVE AS ADJECTIVE	Greta had many posters **to redesign**.

	modifies the verb *laughed*
INFINITIVE AS ADVERB	Mr. Stavros laughed **to forget** his troubles.

INFINITIVE AS ABSOLUTE	**To be blunt,** the paper is plagiarized.

interjection.   A word that expresses emotion or feeling, but that is not grammatically part of a sentence. Interjections can be punctuated as exclamations (!) or attached to a sentence with a comma. Interjections include *oh, hey, wow,* and *well.*

modal auxiliary.   An auxiliary verb that indicates possibility, necessity, permission, desire, capability, and so on. Modal auxiliaries include *can, could, may, might, will, shall, should, ought,* and *must.* (See 25a.)

> Hector **can** write.

> Hector **might** write.

> Hector **must** write.

noun.   A word that names a person, place, thing, idea, or quality. In sentences, nouns can serve as subjects, objects, complements, appositives, and even modifiers.

participle.   A verb form that is used as a modifier (see 25a). The present participle ends with **-ing**. For regular verbs, the past participle ends with **-ed**; for irregular verb forms, the form of the past participle will vary. Participles have the following forms.

To Perform (a regular verb)

PRESENT, ACTIVE   performing

PRESENT, PASSIVE   being performed

PAST, ACTIVE   performed

PAST, PASSIVE   having been performed

Participles can serve as simple modifiers.

> modifies *Officer Bricker*
>
> **Smiling,** Office Bricker wrote the traffic ticket.

However, they often take objects, complements, and modifiers of their own to form verbal phrases, which play an important role in shaping sentences.

> **Writing** the ticket for speeding, Bricker laughed at his own cleverness in catching Arthur.
>
> **Having been ridiculed** often enough in the past by Arthur, Bricker now had his chance for revenge.
>
> Arthur, **knowing** what his friends were doing to Officer Bricker's car, smiled as he took the ticket.

Like an infinitive, a participle can also serve as an **absolute**—that is, a phrase that modifies an entire sentence.

> All things **considered,** the prank was worth the ticket.

parts of speech.   The eight common categories by which words in a sentence are identified according to what they do, how they are formed, where they are placed, and what they mean. Those basic categories are **nouns, pronouns, adjectives, verbs, adverbs, prepositions, conjunctions**, and **interjections**.

preposition.   A word that links a noun or pronoun to the rest of a sentence. Prepositions point out many kinds of basic relationships: *on, above, to, for, in, out, through, by,* and so on. The combination of a preposition and a noun or pronoun produces a **prepositional phrase** such as *on our house, above it, to him, in love, through them, by the garden gate.* (See 25c.)

pronoun.   A word that acts like a noun but doesn't name a specific person, place, or thing—*I, you, he, she, it, they, whom, who, what, myself, oneself, this, these, that, all, both, anybody,* and so on. (See Chapter 22.)

verb. The word or phrase that establishes the action of a sentence or expresses a state of being. (See Chapter 21.)

verb

The music **played** on.

verb

Turning the volume down **proved** to be difficult.

A verb and all its auxiliaries, modifiers, and complements is called the **predicate** of a sentence.

complete subject   predicate

David's band **would have played throughout the night**.

complete subject   predicate

Turning the volume down on the band **proved to be much more difficult than the neighbors had anticipated it might be**.

verbals. Verb forms that act like nouns, adjectives, or adverbs (see Chapter 25). The three kinds of verbals are **infinitives, participles,** and **gerund**s. Like verbs, verbals can take objects to form phrases. But verbals are described as **nonfinite** (that is, "unfinished") verbs because they cannot alone make complete sentences. A complete sentence requires a **finite** verb—that is, a verb that changes form to indicate person, number, and tense.

NONFINITE VERB—INFINITIVE **To have found** security . . .

FINITE VERB I **have found** security.

NONFINITE VERB—PARTICIPLE The actor **performing** the scene . . .

FINITE VERB The actor **performs** the scene.

Credits and Works Cited

Text and Illustrations

Austen, Jane. "Pride and Prejudice," 1813.

Boyer, Ernest L. "Creating the New American College," *The Chronicle of Higher Education,* 1994.

Coles, Robert. *The Moral Life of Children.* New York: Houghton Mifflin, 1986.

Cummings, E. E. From "anyone lived in a pretty how town." Copyright 1940, © 1968, 1991 by the Trustees for the E. E. Cummings Trust, from *Complete Poems: 1904–1962* by E. E. Cummings, edited by George J. Firmage. Reprinted by permission of Liveright Publishing Corporation.

Ehrenreich, Barbara. From "The Economics of Cloning," *Time,* November 22, 1993. © 1993, Time, Inc.

Johnson, Paul. *Intellectuals.* New York: Harper & Row, Inc., 1988, p. 73.

Roland, Alex. "Leave the People Home," *USA Today Online*, July 3, 1997. Reprinted by permission of the author.

Sadker, Myra, and David Sadker. *Failing at Fairness: How Our Schools Cheat Girls.* New York: Touchstone Books/Simon & Schuster, 1994.

Stern, Barbara Lang. "Tears Can Be Crucial to Your Physical and Emotional Health," *Vogue,* June 1979, Condé Nast Publications.

Women in Science. Web pages reprinted by permission of Women in Science at the University of Texas at Austin, <http://www.utexas.edu/students/wis>.

Young, Cathy. "Keeping Women Weak," *NEXT*, Eric Liu, ed. New York: W.W. Norton, 1994.

Photos

2 © Nancy Crampton; 5 Noah Berger/AP/Wide World Photos; 9 Hulton/Archive by Getty Images; 15 © Dorothy Alexander; 23 Photofest; 30 Photofest; 40 Bettmann/Corbis; 47 Hulton/Archive by Getty Images; 51 Hulton/Archive by Getty Images;

Index

Contents